Sphurana

For you – spiritual seeker

Sphurana

The yoga practice of Atma Vichara

Its context and method

Derek Thorne

YOGALIVING

Sphurana – The yoga practice of Atma Vichara – Its context and method

Copyright © 2005 Derek J.Thorne

ISBN: 0-9549571-0-5

First published by Yogaliving Ltd, Timsbury, Bath, England 2005
www.yogaliving.co.uk e-mail: admin@yogaliving.co.uk

Dedicated to my teacher

Bhagavan Sri Ramana Maharshi

and

all seekers of the Self.

Author's note

Irrespective of the ultimate position, this book accepts the fact that for almost everybody, the personality and the workings of the mind dominate conscious life and appear to be who I am. Consequently the writing takes a very specific stance which is to address the practical and the immediate as it appears to seekers. In so doing I am fulfilling a commitment made to articulate teaching which is accessible and directly applicable to current experience. It is from this position that awakening can commence. It is upon this position that we should concentrate and act.

About the author

The insights and detail of instruction within this book result from the direct personal experience of the author who has applied the original and timeless teachings of yoga within himself as student, practitioner and teacher.

Derek Thorne was born in Wales in 1955 and has since childhood experienced a compelling calling towards the spiritual quest. This book is a culmination of that seeking.

In 1997 following more than 20 years of varied yoga practice, he became profoundly drawn to the influence of Sri Ramana Maharshi who emerged directly as his spiritual teacher. The way of Atma Vichara as revealed by Sri Ramana and now applied in a modern context states itself in the fabric of his life.

Derek is married with two children, lives near Bath in England and maintains a full time professional career. He is a gifted teacher, inspirational writer and passionate poet, harmoniously combining the characteristics of working life, family life and spiritual life.

In 2001 he founded the Yogaliving community ashram as a new concept in the development of yoga. Derek gives freely of his time in directing the ashram and its various ongoing projects.

Anyone with a sincere interest in pursuing the teachings within this book is welcome to contact Yogaliving.

www.yogaliving.co.uk

The student and the teacher

Are you my teacher?

Perhaps

May I ask you for guidance, my teacher?

Yes, if you can describe what you want to know

How do I do so, my teacher?

By asking the question

But there is so much to say, so many questions, problems and issues, so many things that fascinate, intrigue and confuse me. What shall I ask?

There is only one question at the core of all your doubts, ask me that

Please tell me what it is?

You would like me to tell you your own question?

Yes, what could it possibly be?

Who am I?

That is the question?

Yes

Shall I ask it now?

Yes, ask it now

Will we answer it together?

Yes, together

Who am I?

CONTENTS

Sangham – The Support of Community

Summary of Approach

Annexes

Glossary

Bibliography

The Teacher's Farewell

Introduction

You are not what you assume yourself to be. Not a body, a mind, a separate individual person with a set of thoughts and ideas. All these things are happening and will continue to happen but they do not define you. Your wholeness is not only these things and is not limited by these things. Your wholeness is the light of awareness in which these things appear. This may be called spirit, or the Self, or I. It can be realised, known and lived.

This is a book for seekers, for each one of those earnest people who experience within themselves the drive to realise spirit directly. For those people who yearn for truth and who, in the face of obstacles and disappointments pursue that yearning persistently. This is a book which presents to those people a careful and comprehensive description of a profound teaching, appearing as a practical way, in glad and mature response to that yearning. The teaching is called Atma Vichara.

Whilst all the work and interpretation that is contained here is the original contribution of the author, none of the core teachings on which it is based are unique or new. They replicate the timeless wisdom of the Vedas, the Upanishads and the profound insights of Sri Ramana Maharshi. Deep respectful acknowledgement is given to the teachings themselves in all their original forms, without which this modern application would be impossible.

In giving and receiving this teaching, together we replicate ancient and well established traditions. It is absolutely the case that you are not alone in your conviction or your seeking. This same interest, this same yearning that you feel, has prompted people throughout history to pursue the spiritual quest and to take action in response to that keenly felt motivation.

I am grateful to understand the teaching of Atma Vichara,

to be living it myself, to have seen its beauty and to now have the opportunity to communicate it to those who choose to seek it out and share it. My particular purpose is to demonstrate that this sadhana is not something which requires special conditions or the renouncing of the world, but is something available and accessible in the forefront of ordinary daily life, as ordinary daily life.

None of this could be possible without the grace, presence and towering influence of my own teacher Bhagavan Sri Ramana Maharshi. He is the lineage and originator by whom I speak and to whom I defer. Particular thanks and recognition is also given to Sri Nisargadatta Maharaj whose parallel position to Sri Ramanas cut through doubts and clarified much in me.

I pledge and commit all my abilities to the modern articulation and continuation of that timeless current by which they shone and by which others shine now.

The traditional invocation for the seeker in yoga and therefore the format selected for the construction of this book is:

- Satyam Sharanam Gachami
  I take refuge in the truth

- Yogam Sharanam Gachami
  I take refuge in yoga

- Guram Sharanam Gachami
  I take refuge in the guru

- Sangham Sharanam Gachami
  I take refuge in the community of practitioners

Om Arunachala Shivaya Namaha
Om Namo Bhagavate Sri Ramanayam

Derek Thorne
Timsbury
January 2005

The credo of truth (satyam)

You exist, you are aware, you know and experience nature.

The power of nature is magnificent, endlessly abundant and creative beyond measure.

The existence of this body and mind that sees and senses, is an intimate part of nature and is not separate from it.

You have done nothing to bring this experience about; it has arisen spontaneously in you.

Action will take place within this experience but you are not the doer of these actions.

You are the presence of awareness in which all actions arise and are known.

This presence is familiar and intimate, fresh and bright; it is called I.

The source from which this state has emerged is *hridayam* – heart or centre.

It is beyond action or personal identity and is the nature of love and being.

This is your true Self – spirit, it does not die.

It is this that you are seeking to know and see.

The seeing of it is being as it, once the false identification as the person is seen and given up.

This is realisation.

The credo of practice (yogam)

Acting in you is the drive to seek and know.

The presence of awareness which experiences this drive can be described as the feeling I.

It is the intimacy of perceiving, direct and prior to thought.

By turning attention to it, this feeling I as itself, reveals itself and expands.

The method of turning is the application of the primary key: "Who am I?"

That which emerges in response is not thought, it is the presence I as itself, knowing itself.

Allowing this and surrendering patiently into this presence of being as I, is the *sadhana* of *Atma Vichara*.

In so doing, seeing beyond what I am not and becoming free of it, is the sadhana of Atma Vichara.

I am not that which seeks, nor the act of seeking; I am that in which seeking arises and in which seeking will end.

This is realisation.

*Satyam
The Truth of
Reality
and Identity*

SATYAM
The truth of reality

Nature

*Have you noticed the fabulous beauty and wonder
of nature?*

For a moment, turn your attention aside from your
routines, your current concerns and interests and consider
the appearance of life, the appearance of nature by which
this life takes place.

This planet on which you sit and live is four and a half
billion years old; it orbits a single star in a galaxy we call the
Milky Way. It constructed itself from gas and dust and has
evolved of itself to be organic and fertile. The diameter of
this galaxy is one thousand light years across and it is
thought to contain one hundred billion other stars. In the
observable universe there are billions of other galaxies,
spreading out across vast and unimaginable distances. The
universe is known to be continuously expanding in all directions. No one can tell you why the universe exists but we
can say that it does and that it has been dynamically
evolving since its magnificent and grand creation some
fifteen billion years ago. Even if theories of creation turn
out to be wrong, the fact that the universe is, and that it
presents itself in any form at all is truly remarkable. Please,
for a moment, reflect on the power behind this. We do not
know what that power is, but we must acknowledge that
whatever it may be, it is staggering, vital and awesome.

Look up at the sky at night, look around you, look anywhere
at the abundance of nature. Consider the intricate dynamics
of biology, of conception and birth, look at mountains,
oceans, trees, flowers and sunlight, the seasons, the orbit of
the moon. Then notice human expression, look at its variety
in art, education, political idealism and technology.

Appreciate your own body and mind, look at its capabilities; it can create, it can interact, it can communicate, it can build, it can feel and experience the world through the sensitivity of its senses. It can work, play, sing and dance, exercise choices and appreciate beauty. It can give kindness and tenderness to others. It is conscious and alive. Its ability to do this has grown from gas and dust, through the creative power of evolution.

Stand back for a moment, put your judgements and personal circumstances to one side and consider these things: the fact that the universe exists, that the world exists, that you exist, consider it objectively just as it is. Anyone who does this sincerely will be thrilled by the wonder of this creation, by its endless and mysterious activity.

Now ask yourself a key question: what have you done to bring this about?

If you ponder this you will conclude that you have done nothing. The magnificence of nature is not dependent for its existence on any action you might take, on the contrary it is carrying you, arising automatically in this moment, happening in this moment, without you having to do anything to support it or sustain it. For you, life in all its complexity and variety has just appeared without any self-determined effort. Nature has been going on like this for a very long time in the formation of stars, the creation of life and the birth of people. All of this momentum and expression is interconnected and nothing is truly independent. You are not a single isolated event; you are part of a continuous and perpetual whole that shapes all its individual parts.

The organism experienced as your person is constructed of chemicals and elements that could not exist without light, heat and the processes of stars. The food that you eat is dependent on atmosphere, rainfall and the labour of people.

The learning that structures your own thought and ideas is the product of social order and the transmission of language. The personal individual actions that you assert now could not be occurring without the existence of your parents, their parents, their parents' parents and the billions of actions that brought them all into being and sustained their lives. Your own life is an intimate part of this dynamic whole, seeded in the creation of the universe, and so are the lives of everybody else. Despite how it may have appeared, or how it feels, you are not and cannot be separate from the progression of events around you. This instrument of body, mind and senses, its place in the world, the energies that move through it, the forces that created it and its characteristics, are particular expressions of nature's whole, of one life.

Now consider something else equally staggering, in terms of individual expression as a human being, you are unique. There is no one else anywhere in the whole of nature who is the same as you. In all the six billion people in the world, not one other looks, thinks, talks, acts and dreams in quite the same way that you do. There are common themes of interest, expression, culture and biology, recognisable trends but there is nothing the same. Just as each snowflake that falls is recognisable as a snowflake but is individual and unique, so that which has arisen as you, is an entirely unique expression of human characteristic and potential.

There can be no mistake to this existence, no accident. You must be here, just as you are, as a unique yet interdependent part of the whole.

Isn't that marvellous?

Is it not entirely obvious that a great power is behind the appearance of nature, that this power is capable of tremendous projection and beauty? It is infinitely grander than anything you have considered before and beyond anything that you can possibly assert?

Arising within this power is the experience of the movement of time.

Time

Before, now and after, is all one beautiful present moment

Despite memory and history which gives the impression of a past, despite aspiration and planning which project a future, if you look carefully at your direct experience of yourself and the world, you will see that there is not an actual past or an actual future that you can point to.

Although the terms before and after are legitimate as concepts, they cannot be touched or reached except in thought, which is itself happening now.

No other moment apart from now exists or could ever exist. It only seems that it does because we witness change and the progression of events, but this change is all appearing within a constant present moment, as is the memory which refers to "before" and the planning which refers to "after".

You are only ever in this immediate present moment. Even if you yourself moved back in time you would still be in your present moment.

This constant moment is however, not static; it is dynamic, fresh, vibrant and alive. Anything can happen in this moment, both predictable and unpredictable. Tremendous forces interact and shape the moment, as the awesome power of creation stretches and plays. This moment is not limited; it is infinite, perpetual and enduring. It is existence itself. To be in any other moment is impossible, for there is no other moment in which to be, however much you might wish it, there is only the fresh presence of now.

This moment, in which all nature appears, is spontaneously occurring. It can be relied upon and trusted to be there, to continue to express, to provide activity and sensation, adventure and experience. There is nothing you have to do to produce this moment; it is producing itself whilst you witness its dynamic play. All that happens is arising in this moment for there is no other place in which experience could exist or be.

To know this clearly and fully places you right in the dynamic presence of your own immediate nature. This is vibrant positive living, in contrast to the stifling tendency of continually missing or denying the moment by dwelling on the past or fretting about the future.

That in which all this experience happens is the mind.

Mind

The beautiful flexibility of the spontaneous mind

You can observe. The very fact that there is observation proves that consciousness exists and that consciousness has the property of knowing. You can think. The very fact that you can think and that thinking exists proves that there is mind. This sensing, seeing, thinking and knowing are present as the living mind in all creatures. However, it is probably only in the cognitive faculties of human beings and other higher animals that the capacity to turn attention towards self-awareness can take place. This is why the humanising of consciousness is seen as very precious, as it allows consciousness to investigate its own nature and origins. The faculty used to do this is the perceiving mind.

At its best what a wonderful tool mind is, full of soaring and magnificent capabilities. At its worst what a burden to carry, full of self-critique and constraint. This can be understood when it is recognised that mind has two fundamental attributes which we can describe as:

• The reactor

• The commentator

The reactive mind is fluid and bright, in the moment and enormously creative. This mind is a fresh contribution to events; it is fit and agile, producing inspiration, information, communication and productivity in response to circumstance as needed. It is clear and alert, natural in its behaviour and not constrained by doubt or fear.

The commentating mind on the other hand dwells in fantasy. It is dull and convoluted in its activities, not of the moment; it is a barrier to spontaneity and flair. The commentating mind is playing in everybody to varying degrees, sifting and analysing events. The dialogue it produces is often of the nature of worry, uncertainty and doubt. It is either rehearsing the future or evaluating the past. It is entirely characterised by our conditioning and is the cause of the mental noise that disturbs the mind.

Can you remember a time when you really experienced periods of free-flowing ideas, when capability was ascendant, when communication was fluid and precise, when your engagement with events was stimulating and uplifting? If you consider these times you will realise that the smoothly reactive mind was confident, automatic and free, taking action effectively and naturally without dwelling on the outcome. At other times the commentating mind prevails, plodding and hesitant, shaping thinking and limiting possibilities through the persistent assertions of either self-protection, inhibition or expectation.

The automatic and fluid play of the reactive mind is the approach to aspire to, freeing the individual from the constraint of either self-importance or self-doubt, which of themselves create the burden of humanity.

Being free of this barrier to freedom and happiness is a primary factor in seeking.

Seeking

I know I am not complete; what is it I want to find?

The force of desire or wanting is prominent and persistent in the mind. The drives that are experienced are often urgent and largely unconscious, having at their root the need for satisfaction. Some desires such as food, love, sex and activity are archetypal and commonly present, whilst others are the result of individual conditioning, but everyone will experience desire, because in myriad ways everyone is searching for completeness. Examine your own life, your moods and your interests, and you can easily verify that throughout your life, the drives and desires you have experienced have at their base this quest for satisfaction, and contentment.

This does not mean that you are not resilient and are not capable of great altruism, selflessness and endurance because of course you are, but if you examine carefully the root of all desire you will conclude that a search for personal happiness or fulfilment is fundamental. If you observe the world you will also see, that in the instincts of people, it is the objects, relationships and sensations of the world, (the sensory and the material) through which this search for happiness is most commonly pursued. Paradoxically it is also entirely evident to all, that despite temporary delights, pleasures derived in this way are unreliable and ultimately unable to satisfy. This does not mean that common pleasures are bad or that they should not be experienced and enjoyed, for that would be foolish. They are part of the beauty of life and they can and will be enjoyed, but it means they are transient in their nature despite our enduring attraction for them.

In some people, the shallowness inherent in this is clearly seen, or at least strongly suspected. There is a growing and perhaps painful recognition, that despite pursuing and enjoying pleasures, enduring satisfaction will not be found there and that there must be something else or somewhere else to look for sustained and satisfying fulfilment.

In those who do see this clearly, a drive for something deeper emerges in the mind and a strong yearning for meaning appears. Symptoms of this are many but will often include dissatisfaction, restlessness and a seeking for the inner secret, the purpose or the truth. Questions such as "Why am I here?" "What is the purpose of life?" etc become prominent and inevitably this brings about an interest in spiritual life however that may be understood. This interest is deep within everyone but may well be dormant or obscured. It is likely to temporarily surface from time to time in all, often during periods of hardship and loss, or by contrast, periods of tenderness and beauty. Some however, are born with this awareness already strongly in place or feel it keenly develop as they mature. For such people their life will be characterised by seeking.

Those who find themselves in the position of seriously studying this book will certainly be in the category of spiritual seeker, that particular quality of desire will be awake in them and will be undeniable. Desire is the basis for all action and this particular desire or yearning is identified in the yoga tradition as highly valuable in that it propels the individual to seek his or her own nature. The texts of yoga recognise and explain this when they speak of the three foundations that need to be in place for spiritual awakening to emerge, mature and blossom:

- *To be born human*

- *To have a longing for liberation*

- *To have access to the teaching and protective care of sages*

Vivekachudamani. v. 3

In this way, the spiritual seeking that you experience in this life and the motivation you feel to respond to it is highly significant. It is seen as evidence of the play of grace within an individual mind, the impulse of evolution and destiny upon you. That is a beautiful and truly precious thing, which despite bringing struggles and frustrations along the way, no one who experiences, would ever want to be without.

To respond to this need effectively you need to apply the force of seeking skilfully in this life.

The place to apply it is here and now, in these immediate current circumstances.

Circumstance

You are where you are because that's the right place to be

This beautiful and marvellous agent of body and mind which you perceive as you is living its life in the only way it is enabled to do so. You must express yourself within the circumstances you find yourself for there is nowhere else for you to be. Even though you may wish for different circumstances, they cannot be different from what they currently are in this moment.

Where you find yourself is a key measure of reality, it is truly here and now and is the place where all is achieved. These circumstances include the potential for freedom, happiness, change, continuity or decline; they must be accepted and not resisted. All possibilities are right here in this moment. You do not need to look elsewhere for some other reality. The presence of this moment and the occurrences which unfold within it are the correct and indeed the only place to be.

You have not made any mistakes in this life that have led to this moment, you have simply acted in the way that expressed and compelled itself in any given circumstance based on the desires and restrictions which define your possibilities. In this moment now, your life is bound to be as it is. It cannot be different and it cannot be as anyone else's.

Crucially however, this moment and the circumstances within it are abundantly alive and contain dynamic options. Not necessarily the options you want or think you deserve but the real and actual options that describe your present and define your potential for growth, expression and positive evolution. These options are not on your terms, they are on nature's terms. Neither are they random; emerging as they do through the interactive moment. Action is fundamental to nature. Action and reaction is bound to take place everywhere and is bound to move in you. The way action takes place here and now will inevitably shape and influence your unfolding circumstance. Some outcomes you will like and some you will dislike but even this choosing and judging is part of nature's play, sifting and shaping events.

The yoga approach is powerful and alive. It allows action and the force of change to take place with engagement and non-resistance. This does not imply absence of effort, for effort and aspiration is the momentum of change. Neither does it imply passive indulgence, for that is contrary to spiritual evolution. What it does imply is engaging in the immediate circumstances and encountering them, not rejecting, denying or avoiding them, nor hoping or dreaming for other circumstances. It implies living in the recognition that all potential for growth and good is contained within these circumstances as they arise now. This approach is descriptive of the spiritual warrior which is further explored in Annex 4.

Whilst aspiring for order, comfort and peace, it is a definite fact that the life histories of many spiritual seekers have been characterised by difficulties, rebellion or struggle. Life may be full of problems, you may feel yourself to be burdened with uncertainties and vulnerabilities and times may be hard. Sometimes it is like this for everybody. We live in a complex world where many competing forces are at large. Clearly society is a stressful place for many but it has always been like this. Although today we have specific modern concerns, throughout history societies have experienced different stresses and threats that, no doubt to the people then, were equally challenging. Difficulties are inevitable and do not mean that you have failed or got things wrong. Indeed, difficulties could be said to be a common and expected feature of life.

One of the observable experiences of spiritual seekers across time is that, discomfort or difficulty is often the propulsion of change; the nourishment if you like by which deeper insights are gained and resistances, which would otherwise limit and condition us, are overcome. Irrespective of what these difficulties are, it is from within the direct encounter with the flourishing immediate circumstances as they emerge, that drive, evolution and clear perception has its birth. It is within this birth that all restrictions will be absorbed and all freedoms attained. It is within the opposite (denial and avoidance) that stagnation, inertia and the repetition of old conditioning prevails.

So much angst is created by non-acceptance of our circumstances and by wishing and hoping for different arrangements or by always expecting things to be on our terms. This way is pointless and leads to disappointment and despair. Instead of doing this take the opposite stance, be as you are. Allow the aspirations you feel for love and tolerance to mature and watch the changing play as your life dynamically unfurls. The creative instrument you see as your person is meant to be here, as much a part of nature as any other life, there is a part to play and an expression to make, and that must and will happen. You can be sure that where the forces of productivity progression or assertion are needed, they will arise, when they are not apparent, then things will remain as they are until circumstance works its way out and change inevitably appears.

Sri Nisargadatta Maharaj put it controversially but perfectly when he said in his book "I Am That":

"Want what you have and don't want what you don't have. Then you will be happy."

But who is it that is experiencing circumstance? What is the truth of identity?

The truth of identity

Where is experience?

Nothing is without, all is within

Consider your own direct experience, in each waking moment and during dreams, you are experiencing events in the form of senses, memories, thoughts and behaviours. Some of these events feel as if you are observing them and some feel as if you are participating in or directing them. Some will appear internal and some external, but if you put all these distinctions to one side and if you look carefully, you will see that irrespective of what the event is, all that you know and are aware of is being experienced within perception. Where is this perception?

The body as a sensing instrument exists in nature, bringing about this experience of world and thought. The body moves about in space, carrying the senses with it. When the body is in England, England is displayed, when the body is in India, India is displayed. So clearly that which is seen and felt has an intimate relationship with the body. But all events, even if they are perceived as being in the space outside the body only have existence inside a perceiving you that knows.

Consider dreams, in dreams there is no solid body, no sensing instrument moving in space, yet there is a rich and real landscape of experience that whilst you are dreaming is indistinguishable from waking. Whole worlds are apparent in your dream which have tangible reality and perspective, yet there is no external physics by which they are created. What is seen in dreams, as in waking, is happening inside perception, inside a consciousness that is in union with a body and mind, acting as a receiving and expressing instrument for it. In this sense you are not within the world in the way that you have thought but on the contrary, the whole experienced world is within the perceiving consciousness of you.

17

The only thing that prevents the easy recognition of this is the conviction that you are inside the body, mind and brain which seems to identify and define you. From that position clearly the above statements make no sense, but you are not the body, or rather not only the body, as the body is also an experienced event happening within perception, within consciousness.

This consciousness is much bigger and more spacious than you had thought possible. All things arise in it, the day as it appears, sleep, dreams and memory, thoughts and feelings, the body, this life and all its events.

Even though from the perspective of geometry the statement "I am over here and you are over there" is legitimate. Here, there and everything else, every detail, every action can only be known and seen within the consciousness that knows it. The total field of events appears within and nothing is external.

The body is called a field Arjuna
He who knows it is called the Knower of the field
I am the Knower of the field in everyone
Knowledge of the field and its Knower is true knowledge
                                    Bhagavad Gita ch.13 v.1

So what is it that is acting in this field?

What is acting?

Life is acting in you, you are being lived

Think back through the incidents of your life, through the roles you have played, the interests you have had, the things you have wanted to find out, the experiences that have attracted you and the behaviours you have applied. In the time of their arising and the fullness of their pursuit, these activities have seemed singular and individual to you, they have seemed like your own personal endeavours, self-created. They have felt like separate, private and individual ideas motivated and generated by you, independently through personal choice.

But look around, can you see that other people are also ful-filling these same impulses, acting out these same behav-iours, pursuing these same interests in just the way that you do? Not exactly the same as you, for that is impossible, but similar. Different hands, different faces but similar functions.

The impulses and reactions that run through your mind are part of a whole, part of the enduring themes and potentials of nature expressing herself, of which this body is a part, and cannot be separated. There is no possibility that actions can be said to be entirely self-generated and independently created by you as yours.

This is the meaning of the essential yet beguiling statement made frequently in *Vedanta* – "You are not the doer".

The style and detail of the interests that arise in you are the product of *karma*. It is seeded in the past and is in no way random. Neither can it be denied. There may be creativity, there may be inspiration, there may be dullness, constraint or difficulty. You do not have choice as to what appears. The function of choice is how you react in the moment of its arising, and that choosing itself is also constrained by the conditioning and intelligence that boundaries the mind and limits actions.

It may not seem like this because you have been taught that you are in charge, you have been taught that you are the independent chooser of choices, the doer of actions. But there is no chooser who stands alone, separate from events, who has the freedom to act entirely independently or who can freely choose the thoughts and feelings that appear. There is only thought arising and reaction taking place within the context of memory and the themes of conditioning, by which the personality that frames you is shaped. You can do everything you want to do but you cannot do anything there is to do.

Nonetheless the everyday experience is that when demands and responsibilities are present, they are keenly felt and owned as mine. Activity takes place, thinking develops, decisions are reached and action is applied. You feel you are the source and centre of these processes, organising it and doing it. Obviously there is an instrument of body and mind which does engage and is doing it, but what is the force which provokes it and who directs it? Try to look closely as to what exactly it is that you feel this doer of actions and chooser of choices to be and you will conclude that it is a combination of observation, memory and a particular mental characteristic called will. It is this will that is the director, the chooser, the apparent stage manager of events, the organiser, the driver, the commander and the critic. This will is the decision maker and the restrainer; it plays actively in the affairs of the moment, it dominates and conducts the mental life. It is this will that states "I want this" and "I want that". It is this wilful thinker with whom you have identified and which assumes the role of me for most people.

If you look closely and patiently however, you will see that this will is not the most direct centre of you, not the first principle because as an object it is also perceived and known. It is not that which first arises, as it is itself an arrangement of thought and instinct happening within a larger and more spacious me.

The will also changes. When you are dreaming, willing is present, as is thought and observation but its characteristics and form are altered because memory and continuity are not present. From where has this dreaming will arisen? From where does the waking will arise?

The majority position is to feel that there is a person at the centre, that this person is the doer and that this doer is who I am; a self-directing thinker that feels, deduces and acts. Commonly this is taken for granted, it is not thought about or looked at but once you do, it becomes very clear that although all this is happening, you are not this me, not this doer of actions; for there is no personal doer of actions in the way you have assumed it. There is just doing arising, happening, and being experienced or known by consciousness. All the yoga texts state and promise that this assumed me is not the foundation of who you are. It is an appearance, an arisen activity. The doing is happening by itself, an expression of that wondrous *shakti* which in various ways digests your food, heals your wounds, runs your senses and provides your memories and thoughts. This power is being experienced by a greater nature. We may call this greater nature spirit, I, the Self or the light of man.

The king questioned the sage Yajnavalkya:

Yajnavalkya, what is the light of man?
The sun is our light your majesty, for by that light we sit,
    work, go out and come back.
When the sun sets, what is the light of man?
Then the moon is our light, for by that we sit, work, go out
    and come back.
When the sun sets and the moon sets, what is the light of
    man?
Then fire is our light, for by that we sit, work, go out and
    come back.

*When the sun sets and the moon sets and the fire goes out,
what is the light of man?*

*Then speech is our light, for by that we sit, work, go out and
come back.*

*When the sun sets and the moon sets and the fire goes out
and no one speaks, what is the light of man?*

*The Self indeed is the light of man, for by that we sit, work,
go out and come back.*

Who is that Self?

*The Self, pure awareness, shines as the light within the
heart, surrounded by the senses, only seeming to think,
seeming to move, the Self neither sleeps, wakes nor
dreams.*

Brihadaranyaka Upanishad ch.4 v.2-7

What then is this light of man? Who am I?

Who am I?

Living as the answer to this question is spiritual awakening

Throughout your life, through all the changing events and roles something has been constant. That thing is the very state of being alive, the state of existence, the ability to see and recognise that I am and I know. This something is not thinking, it is consciousness itself. It is that which arises each morning from sleep as the presence I.

All the events and roles, moods and behaviours, knowledge, opinions and actions related to the personality have changed but this I state has not. What was it that looked out of the two year old, the eighteen year old, the thirty year old, the fifty year old, the eighty year old and so on? It was consciousness itself. Of course the perspective has changed, the interests have changed, the thinking has changed, the behaviour has changed but consider carefully and you will see that the enduring power of awareness which is prior to all these things and which sustains all these things has not changed. It is this which has continuously stated itself as the first principle I, without break or gap, and it is this which is responsible for your familiarity and aliveness upon which changing experience, changing body, growth and maturity have overlaid themselves. All the experiences, events and occurrences that appear as this life, all of them including the sensing person itself and the identification that goes with it, have arisen within this knowing power. It is this knowing power which can be described as spirit, Self or I.

I is not a person, I is the power of knowing which lights the person and makes the functioning of person possible; not a body but a presence of being. Everything that is known, irrespective of geography, geometry, distance and time, is seen through and within this presence of being.

In the city of Brahman is a secret dwelling, the lotus of the heart. Within this dwelling is a space and within that space is the fulfilment of our desires. What is within that space should be longed for and realised. As great as the infinite space beyond is the space within the lotus of the heart. Both heaven and earth are contained in that inner space, both fire and air, sun and moon, lightning and stars. Whether we know it in this world or know it not, everything is contained in that inner space. Never fear that old age will invade that city; never fear that this inner treasure of all reality will wither and decay. This knows no age when the body ages; this knows no dying when the body dies. This is the real city of Brahman; this is the Self, free from old age, from death and grief, hunger and thirst. In the Self all desires are fulfilled.

Chandogya Upanishad ch.8 v.1.1-1.5
(Easwaran page 191)

The city of which this reference speaks is hridayam, the centre, the spiritual heart and source; it is the prevailing awareness within which all manifestation has emerged. This is not the sense of being a person which structures this life, nor can it be personalised. It is spirit, the essence of life, within which the person has temporarily appeared.

Indeed it is not just the yoga texts which say this, as a similar recognition is the common thread in all spiritual and religious understanding. Those who pursue spiritual enquiry seriously from whatever tradition they are cultured in, reach common experience and realisations. One example of this would be the statements of Meister Eckhart, a medieval mystic who grew up in a Christian tradition and spoke clearly regarding the essence, immediacy and intimacy of spirit:

"If the soul were stripped of all her sheaths God would be discovered all naked to her view and would give himself to her withholding nothing. As long as the soul has not thrown off all her veils, however thin, she is unable to see God. Any

medium, but a hair's breadth, in between the body and the soul stops actual union."

Eckhart quoted by Fleming, 1988, pg 47.

The reason you feel restless or dissatisfied is because you are yearning for the enduring satisfaction that you sense is available somewhere but has been inaccessible throughout your life. What you are yearning for is to know yourself, to experience the end of the feeling of separation and the re-establishment with the fullness of your true nature. All the yoga texts describe that nature as *satchitananda*, as love, beauty and peace. It is that which is at the basis of our search for happiness, in all the hopes and dreams of the world this is the contentment that we really want.

To have that, we need to let go of what we have become and to wake up to what we already are but do not see. It is that change in perception and consciousness which describes awakening, enlightenment or self-realisation. Awakening is the reorientation of identity from that which you thought you were, to the recognition of that which you truly are. It is not the thinking mind which does this. Awakening comes upon you slowly; it is not created from the position of the individual trying for something. It is only enabled through absorption, surrender and the *Sphurana* of experiential insight.

To enable this we need a route, a way, a practice. We need to know what the practice is and how to approach it.

We need knowledge of the skilful application of sadhana.

Sadhana

Sadhana is my jewel, my life, my work, my refuge

Sadhana is a *Sanskrit* word meaning practice. It is descriptive of method and approach. It is the application of yoga technique. Sadhana is what you do to realise your goal. It is the essence of the yogic path.

Amongst the wide variety of techniques and approaches that exist there is a clear and profound way of self-enquiry which in Sanskrit is termed Atma Vichara. It is profound for this reason.

The Self, our true and enduring nature, is not the thinking person, yet we experience ourselves now as a person, with the skills and faculties of a thinking person. How can those skills and faculties be used to realise something which is outside of them?

Sri Ramana Maharshi answered this very incisively in the following key *sloka*:

In the centre of the Heart-Cave, Brahman shines alone.
It is the form of Self experienced directly as I-I.
Enter the heart through self-enquiry, or merging, or by breath-control and become rooted as that.

Ramana Gita ch. 2.v.2

The second line of this verse is of tremendous importance. It states that the transcendental Self is, within these human faculties, experienced in the form I-I directly. The reason it is described as I-I rather than I, is to indicate the perpetual and spontaneous continuity of that power, untainted, non-objectified and non-personalised, the purity of being as being. This means that the form I-I or rather the feeling and presence I, is the very light of the Self (the light of man). Its very structure and essence is the radiance of the Self. By understanding what this means and by turning attention into this presence I, that which is looking and thinking (the person) becomes absorbed into the presence I, and identification transforms from person to I itself. Further absorption into the source and depth of that presence brings about the recognition that I am not the doer, the end of identification as a separate ego and unification in non-personal identity as the Self (satchitananda). That is not so much something to do or achieve, it is rather something to submit to and allow.

An absolutely fundamental point to realise is this: You exist as the Self now, you already are what you seek but you do not see it, feel it, or know it. This is because of the sense of identity as doer, as the separate person, that has strongly and persistently arisen, declaring itself as I. Experiencing change in that position from that which you have become to that which you truly are, is sadhana. The method and approach is called Atma Vichara.

"To keep the mind constantly turned within and to abide in the Self, is alone Atma Vichara (self-enquiry)."
Sri Ramana Maharshi

The following chapters now present a description of this practice and its detailed application within everyday life.

Yogam
The Sadhana
of Practice

YOGAM
The sadhana of practice

The practice of Atma Vichara

The objective is to stabilise attention in the felt awareness of the natural and spontaneous presence of being, shining directly as I.

Sit quietly, relax and become still. Let your attitude become gentle, easy and soft. In this moment there is no doubt that you are aware, it is natural and obvious. As you sit, any kind of experience may come into this awareness; sensations in your body, information through the senses, memories, thoughts, moods and feelings. All of these things are part of the play of events. They can be allowed to rise and fall, but let yourself become disinterested in them, don't follow them with your interest.

Irrespective of what the events are, there is something else in this moment, something constant, which is here now and which endures perpetually. It is not something new to find, it is something to be accepted as already here. This something is direct, familiar and full; it is all around, continuous, without break or gap. It presents as your very being. It is the peace of the moment, the feeling I exist, the feeling of being awake, the silent presence of being.

Remain steady and pose the question **"Who am I?"** ask that question once or twice. Do not expect an intellectual answer. In posing the question, a current of attentiveness is set up which enables you to simply recognise that you are not the body, nor the events, you are closer than that, more intimate than that, existing as the presence of being, the feeling I.

Recognise that feeling, it is the presence that has been constant every second throughout your whole life, but to which you have never turned your interest. Turn your interest there now, rest it there and be still with it. Hold your attentiveness in this stillness, with this presence of being. You are not meditating on an object, you are not trying to find something, you are being the subject. When all things cease, this subject remains, when all thoughts subside, this subject remains. Learn to be steady with this; learn to be less and less distracted and to be still with this, attentive and alert.

When your attention drifts, periodically put the question, "Who am I?" again. This brings you back to the awareness of the presence of being. When thoughts arise to disturb you, ask **"Who knows these thoughts?"** then again you will recognise they are appearing within the power of knowing; within the presence of being that presents as the feeling I. It is this into which our attention is absorbed.

Beyond that, there is nothing else to actively do except relax, be patient, surrender and when the feeling I is clear, with alert awareness consider **"From where has this I arisen?"** you are not thinking about it nor trying to find an answer to understand, you are instead allowing yourself to merge into the centre of your own source.

This is the practice of Atma Vichara.

Be private and persistent in your approach, be very patient, seek guidance to steer you and remove doubts. Seek the company of others to support you.

Summary of practice

The essence of tapas

There are two commonly used words in Sanskrit that mean practice, one is sadhana the other is *tapas*. Knowing exactly what practice is and being clear about it is essential for progress. Sri Ramana put it perfectly when in 1907 he was asked by Ganapati Muni "What is tapas?" His answer is brilliant:

"If one watches from whence the notion I arises the mind is absorbed in that.
That is tapas."

Sri Ramana Maharshi

Serious students of Atma Vichara should dwell deeply on this *sutra*. For those who choose to look, within this statement, is the totality of method.

In other responses to questions he identified three specific agents of practice – 3 keys. They can be summarised as:

The 3 keys

❖ Put the question **"Who am I?"**

❖ When thoughts arise ask **"Who knows these thoughts?"**

❖ When the feeling I is clear ask **"From where has this I arisen?"**

To the practitioner these are as valuable as precious jewels. They are tremendously important and secure aids. They are anchors in sadhana. They will not fail and if persistently applied they will take you to your goal. Clearly they are questions but none of them are expected to provoke intellectual answers. In that sense they do not have answers, but they do have resolutions. They are triggers which, when applied cause attention to turn around into itself and steadily absorb back into the subject, which presents itself as the feeling I am. This absorption is characterised by a loosening of the identification me as a person, a subduing of the seeking through thinking, a reduction in thought movement and the passive acknowledgement that it is the consciousness I am, that more closely defines I than the body, thoughts and feelings. This consciousness has itself emerged from a deeper source, it is that source-spring to which we surrender and into which we merge. The spring is hridayam.

The following sections elaborate extensively on the detail of practice and how it can be applied.

Guram Guidance and Teaching

GURAM
Guidance and teaching
Commentary on practice

Let my practice be skilful and clear

There is no doubt if you sincerely pursued the question "Who am I?" rigorously, you would come to the conclusion that you cannot be defined as the body, the mind, the thoughts or the events that you experience. These things are happening but they are arising in something, something which is enduring and constant, something which is closer than the things themselves. That something is the power of awareness, within which the world arises and is variously experienced. It is that power which constitutes I. It is that power which is present all the time and in all circumstances as your very substance.

Philosophically we may already know this and can state "I am the power of awareness, being itself". Although this is good to know intellectually it does not really help as long as it remains a concept, it is then no more than another mental object, an idea, it is simply more thinking to dwell upon and ponder. The sadhana of Atma Vichara requires more than this as it aims to experientially realise the subject directly in first person, felt experience. It is the bright recognition and subsequent acceptance of the subject, not as an idea but as a direct state, and the passive abidance as that power which is the entire focus of practice.

Atma Vichara is a meditation discipline and an easy everyday lifestyle. The sadhana is beautiful, delicate, potent and profound. It is a reorientation from the identification of what you thought you were to the recognition of who you are. While simple in its concept and approach, it demands patience in its application as it requires you to recognise the substance within which thought and identity is arising.

This involves incisive and courageous discrimination through the structures of ego that have veiled the mind for so long.

Through enquiring *"Who am I?"* the feeling I am which is obvious but was previously unseen, becomes recognised and immediate. Dwelling in that recognition, allowing it and accepting it without distraction or deviation, is the practice. It could be described as becoming absorbed in stillness. This is not something achieved by forced effort; it is something which emerges through its own power. The term absorption is important as it highlights the key distinction in Atma Vichara from other meditation approaches. You do not retain the position of a witness looking at the stillness, for as Sri Ramana said, you cannot have one self looking at another self, there is only one. As thinking subsides and the current of I increases, it becomes clearer that the feeling I am is the first and most intimate state accessible to the conscious mind, it is the subject, it is not the object, it is the immediate bright presence, the feeling of stillness within which identity rises independent of thought.

To bring this about you need to discover how to surrender attention, how to turn away from the common pathways of thinking and accept a meditative position of alert and potent being rather than active doing. One of the obstacles to enabling this to happen is the strong tendency of the mind to seek and hunt, to look and want and then to commentate on what we find or what we can't find. The mind wants to look out and analyse, it wants to have an object to consider, it wants to look at something other than itself, it wants to think. Your tendency throughout your life has been to dwell in these processes and to support them through identifying with them. When someone says to you "Put the question who am I?" you think; when someone says "Find the feeling I and reside there" you hunt. This tendency exists as a result of our conditioned nature, our strong enduring belief that I am this person that thinks and acts (the doer). Consequently when you sit with this practice, there is an urgency which arises in the mind. It's a familiar urgency, it populates your days. It's the urgency of wanting to work it out, of wanting to think it through, of wanting to seek and experience, of wanting to find an answer. In doing this and without knowing it, you are perpetuating the identification with the doer. In Atma Vichara the answer does not come through this route. All of that common and familiar habit of analysis and probing ideas is not the place to apply your interest. All of that activity is nothing other than more thinking and the creation of more concepts. It continues to support the ego, the very thing that stands in the way of realisation, and has no hope of transcending it.

You have to learn to drop this urgency to do and get. In its place you remain attentive to the presence I, to the presence of this feeling I, without thinking about it. To be with it, to stay there, to accept and with bright alertness to surrender into that immediate presence of being. That is the practice.

Remember you are being the subject, you are not watching an object.

For some time the mind may struggle against this and it is likely that you will be seeking for the feeling I as a new thing. The mind will have to exhaust this tendency through patient persistence as it unlearns its habits and eventually quietens down. In that quietness there is the feeling I, it was there all the time but you were preoccupied with the thinking, once the thinking dwindles, the urgency to seek pacifies and the feeling I is increasingly obvious. It could be best described as:

The radiance of awareness.

The direct presence of being.

Some other descriptions that may help you accept its reality are:

- Aliveness
- Being awake
- The state of existence
- That which is there when thinking stops
- The familiarity I am
- Beingness
- Stillness
- Fullness

How do you know when you have the feeling I right?

First of all accept that this practice emerges and strengthens over time. You will not be able to confirm it, or be secure in your application of it all at once. Its presence may not be perceived when you first start to practice, but actually persisting in the face of that, is in itself part of the discrimination, as the mind's activity unlearns old habits and more subtle insights are seen.

The feeling I cannot be described in the way you want it to be described, because it is not a new thing to find. It is something that already is but is currently weakly perceived. It is the very centre of your nature, the subject within which everything is known. It is the consciousness that you are right now, but you do not appreciate or recognise.

You cannot see the Seer of seeing. You cannot hear the Hearer of hearing. You cannot think the Thinker of thinking. You cannot understand the Understander of understanding. He is your Self, which is everything.
Brihadaranyaka Upanishad ch.3. v.4.2

The feeling I is not an object of thinking in terms of a line of thought, or a piece of understanding. It is not an opinion you hold, or something you can achieve. The feeling I is not an object of feeling in terms of a tactile sensation that can be examined by the thinker. The feeling I is a tangible pervading state of being. Tangible in the sense that it is recognisable and known through its own power, but so ordinary, familiar and all pervading, that you miss it. At first it could be said to be peace and quiet or silence. When you start to recognise it, by allowing yourself to appreciate its presence, then it grows in stature, and becomes more apparent, more alive, recognition is more natural and vibrant. It deepens and increasingly reveals itself right at the centre, as the subject, because it is yourself. The change is, we stop thinking about it and instead be as it, basking in that natural being.

This is not something that can possibly be achieved from the perspective of the will that has it, or finds it, or gains it. That very structure of identity from which you have traditionally thought, analysed and looked must allow itself to quieten and recede. It is truly the case, as already discussed, that the common sense of identity (I am the thinker and doer) is a false assumption. In its progressive absence is the familiarity of silent being. It is the very radiance of that being which arises of itself, to state itself as I. This happens slowly through the compliance of the will in turning away from itself and is only achieved through patient practice.

What is it that knows the feeling I?

This is an essential and subtle point. As hinted at above there are not two selves, one looking at the other. What there is, is thinking, all the activities of the mind, and the power within which these things, whatever they may be, are seen. It is this power itself which is the presence I. That which knows it, is it itself, by its own power. Its very essence is inherently self-aware. But what does self-aware mean? It does not mean thinking and understanding, it means direct knowing through the power of being itself, as itself. Being – consciousness, simply is, and reveals itself obviously and naturally when other associations are removed and crucially when the sense I am the thinking person is given up. This is why negation was a traditional Vedic teaching known as *neti, neti* (not this, not this). When everything else, every secondary object is removed, the singular first subject (awareness) is, by itself, with no effort you have to make, effortless being.

That soul is not this, it is not that (neti, neti). It is unceasable for it cannot be ceased. It is indestructible for it is not destroyed. It is unattached for it does not attach itself. It is unbound, it does not tremble, it is not injured.
                              Brihadaranyaka Upanishad ch.2 v.3.6

Realise that to be Brahman (the Self) which is non-dual, indivisible, one and blissful, which is indicated as the irreducible substratum after the negation of all tangible objects.
                              Self Knowledge v 56

Who is it that practices?

It is the ego that practices. Something motivates this particular person to become a seeker and to pursue that seeking through sadhana. Part of our conditioning wants to see beyond itself which, ironically perhaps, means the end of the ego's reign. There is a certain property, a certain shakti within consciousness that prompts this. It may also indicate why spiritual practice can often feel difficult as if we are struggling against ourselves, well in a way we are. The ego naturally wants to assert itself, to promote itself, to sustain itself, there are strong drives within humanity that do just that, yet in some, the urge to become free of the ego arises and spiritual seeking begins. It is likely that this is an inherent feature of evolution, the extension and inevitable outcome of natures design so to speak. In any event it is the ego that practices, not the Self. The Self lights the practice along with everything else and reveals itself as itself as practice matures and eventually ends.

How often should I practice?

The answer is often. This requires effort in the short and medium term but becomes increasingly automatic and effortless as familiarity develops. It is however important to understand what practice means and you should make three distinctions:

• **Focused practice**

This is where you sit still without other activity and meditate on the three keys and the beingness that prevails. Yoga practitioners will recognise this as *dhyana* practice. Become familiar with doing this often for both short and longer periods. Fifteen minutes in the morning or evening, five minutes on the train or bus, two minutes in between jobs at your desk or place of work, on waking up in the morning for a few moments etc. Longer periods means arranging a sitting during your week when you can, depending on your maturity and experience, extend both the duration and intensity of practice for up to an hour.

In addition, periodically sit with your teacher and/or other *sangha* friends for communal sadhana. There is no doubt at all that this significantly strengthens the current of practice. Whilst taking the above approach, do not become too precious or rigid, you are in this for the long term. Practice needs to be easy and welcoming, not a burden or a tense effort. If it becomes so you may as well drop it for that moment and go and do something else. A persistent chipping away and a gradual familiarisation rather than austere confrontation is the most practical course for most (but not all). Whilst regularity is good, it mustn't become dry or mechanical. It really doesn't matter if you miss sessions, just pick it up again later but do pick it up again. Where possible, once or twice a year organise retreat for yourself, where you can concentrate on deeper and longer practice without distraction.

• **Common practice**

As you go about your days remain mindful of who is acting, who walks, who works, who thinks, who organises and plans, who drives, who shops, who makes breakfast, etc etc. This is not some deep analysis to depersonalise you from the world, it is a light, easy and friendly thing, allowing you to realise that you are truly not the doer. Doing is happening automatically even in its most intimate parts. You are the knower, the being in which doing, seeing and acting appears. This, you will find, brings an absolute fascination to life, an easy acceptance of the dynamic play of the world and an increasingly relaxed non-attachment with no loss of productivity or capability. You are able to just let everything get on with itself including your own initiatives and personal responsibilities. There is no denial here; there is by contrast a beautiful freedom.

• Study

When convenient, when you have spare moments to reflect, read the important core texts that have become meaningful to you. My own advice as to what these can be is given in Annex 9. Also meet with others, speak with others about the practice, spend time in easy company with those who think like you, talk and share, and access your teacher from time to time.

The approach of passive alertness

Through the developing skill of redirecting awareness away from mental habits, the appreciation of the power I will become directly felt rather than thought. Your practice is then the allowing of the feeling I to emerge and reveal itself through its own radiance in the quiet absence of thoughts, but this does not mean doing nothing; it does not imply a vacant absence.

The quality of attention you apply is soft but alert, relaxed but vital, strong but tender. This silent allowing is full of energy and liveliness and this liveliness is created by using the three keys. The questions themselves stimulate an inward sensing, a momentum of awareness receding into itself. This is in no way dull, empty or vacant; it is by contrast full of power and brightness. In this sense it is focused and intense, not vague in any way. However the other extreme is also to be avoided. This is not a practice of hard, forced attention, as that is only created when you are trying to make something happen through your own will. This is a delicate practice; the only hard part is becoming familiar with what it is and how to enable it by turning away from thinking. Beyond that the requirement is for earnest, persistent and patient practice only. When this is applied, a deepening familiarity with the feeling I will emerge of itself, not because you have made it happen but because you have not impaired its revealing through thinking. Your duty then is to surrender into that, to merge into that, to give up the prominence of the probing thoughts and to merge attention into the immediate central feeling of the heart's presence. In this way you shine as you are, and take rest from what you are not. You must be alert and focused but gentle in your approach, relaxed in your manner, passively, patiently alert.

Feeling not thinking

A key point to appreciate and fully accept is that the realising of the state I is more in the realm of feeling or sensing than it is of thinking. It is the very first place and first moment of you, it is right here stating itself as I, and that is not an experience felt or seen from inside the directional looking of the probing mind. It is softer than this, more current than this, thinking will not find it because thinking has arisen in it and is known by it. Thinking is a distraction to its revealing. If you find yourself thinking, this is interfering with the practice, if you pursue boredom or agitation, this is interfering with the practice, if you analyse and compare, this is interfering with the practice. All these actions are distractions. The practice is being still, steady and attentive in the immediate conscious space which is constant throughout. It is present prior to any of these actions arising and it will be present when each of them fall and change. You are not the watcher watching the space from a point of analysis (that is thinking) you are the conscious space itself or more accurately the source from which that space has sprung.

All this, and the deepening beyond, has to be approached intimately and directly, it has to be experienced and faced, as well as being talked about and read about. It is a personal adventure, a direct and intimate encounter approached patiently in the private silent space of your own awareness. Through asking "Who am I?" the sense of being the separate watcher, watching and waiting ends, and the direct sense of being, in first person, right at the first person centre, expands.

Expectation

A key barrier which causes tension in so much sadhana is expectation. This is the force which leads us to anticipate the appearance of change and experience on our own terms. It leads us to having a concept, even though it may be a vague concept, of what's going to happen. An expectant attitude establishes itself strongly in the mind and without meaning to, we are looking, seeking, hunting and waiting for a particular thing or event to occur. It will be obvious to you, if you consider it, that succumbing to this approach maintains the ego's stance. You remain identified as the looker, looking for the thing you hope to find or see which will always be in the realm of the familiar or the imagined. What this does is limit the new and set up a constraint which is a strong barrier to surrender. The subtleties of emergence can never arise in these conditions.

Similarly it is a hindrance to expect to emulate or replicate the experiences and perspectives which we read about in the books written by masters of yoga. The reality is that the attainment of the *jnani* is comparatively rare and it is not this that should be anticipated or sought. The method of the jnani, is however, not rare and can be pursued by everybody who is drawn to it.

Here is a real insight, it is the application of the method

which is the focus and the commitment, what then emerges as a result of the method is direct, personal and intimate to you. It is that which is real and not the expected or imagined.

You are a regular practitioner, an ordinary person with your own destiny, you are not a saint. Awakening for you will (probably) not be of the same order as the great seers and you should fundamentally accept that. In so doing it will immediately protect you from frustrations that can otherwise impair practice. Some of the biggest stresses in life come from trying to be more than we are, or trying to do more than we can cope with. You, like everyone else, are in God's hands and it seems that the precise detail of how practice is experienced by a person and how that practice impacts specifically upon an individual mind is variable.

Talk to your teacher and your fellow practitioners about method and glean from that the common themes of approach, but do not expect to get it right in comparison to how it is exactly reported by another. The only thing to get right is the establishment for yourself of the *Sphurana* in you, to keep returning to that current, and abandon all controls and assumptions to that current. There is no doubt that it can be trusted and no doubt that its movements will stabilise in you. The approach to take is to surrender to that and not try to organise that into a set of characteristics that you have read about, expect or wish for.

An evolution not an event

Another mistake to clarify is the assumption that in the practice of Atma Vichara you are trying to achieve the result in that meditation session. This is the wrong approach. Each time you bring your attention to the feeling I you are strengthening the current which percolates slowly and progressively through your life. It is an evolving emergence, naturally occurring through the participation of your willingness to surrender the ego and focus on the presence of the heart. It develops; it is not a single event. Focused meditation practice is the right base by which you give yourself the opportunity to overcome resistances and clarify the current of awareness. In this sense it is required and essential but as already pointed out it is not the only base. At any time and in any appropriate circumstances, asking yourself who works, who acts, who thinks, who feels, will contribute to increasing the obvious recognition that I am not the body and I am not the thoughts, I am not the actions, I am the witness to all that occurs, I am the shining and enduring consciousness that states itself intimately. I am that now, and I continue to be that. Whilst seated meditation will form a cornerstone of your routine, it is not the entirety of the practice and it does not define the event in which realisation will happen.

Patience and consistency

To develop any ability and to perfect any skill, practice is required. One of the observable weaknesses in the common pursuit of yoga is that practice is often diverse and dilute. It is not unusual for yoga practitioners to move from thing to thing and style to style, often repeating this tendency for decades. Although offering variety and a response to the urge to seek, such an approach will not deliver enduring results and will inevitably remain superficial. Similarly, practice is often inconsistent and approached haphazardly, as few are able to sustain the personal discipline required to instil new habits, within the context of distractions and avoidance.

There is no doubt that spiritual practice requires patience and skilled application. All of these things rely on motivation and persistence. Results do not come all at once, enduring and sustained effects are not apparent in the early weeks, months or even years. It is important to accept that real change takes place through maturity and over a whole lifetime. For almost everybody there is no way to avoid this, neither should we try, it is simply the way nature is. Indeed there is a certain beauty in the commitment, expressed through determination and faith, which keeps you going. Even though it may not feel like it, the very fact that this interest and motivation is present is evidence of grace working within your mind.

This will not be the case for all; the capacity to avoid dilution and diversion in practice will not appear in all, indeed it is said in yoga that four qualifications have to be in place for the *sadhak* before practice can be seriously pursued. These are:

- *The willingness to discriminate between the real and the unreal*
- *Non-attachment or dependence on the fruits of one's own actions*
- *The 6 virtues:*
  - *Tranquillity*
  - *Self-control*
  - *Withdrawal*
  - *Forbearance*
  - *Faith*
  - *Concentration on the Self*
- *Intense yearning for liberation*

Vivekachudamani v. 19

Similarly Patanjali, who, as a great leader and authority in yoga practice, is unambiguous when he says to us clearly:

"Practice is firmly grounded only when it is pursued properly for a long time without interruption."

Yoga Sutra ch.1 v.14

Sri Ramana gave the most excellent response to one questioner who was asking how to proceed for the long term amidst the setbacks and difficulties that inevitably arise in sustained practice:

Questioner
When an endeavor is made to lead the right life and to con-
centrate thought on the Self there is often a downfall and
break, what is to be done?
"It will come all right in the end.
There is the steady impulse of your determination that sets
you on your feet again after every downfall and break.
Gradually the obstacles are all overcome and your current
becomes stronger, everything comes right in the end. Steady
determination is what is required."

Sri Ramana Maharshi

Knowing this helps you, it ensures you accept the privilege, the beauty and duty of being born a spiritual seeker and that you apply sadhana with patience and eagerness. Despite this it is pointless to force and overdo practice or to adopt rigid routines that make your life miserable. This leads to an arid and sometimes arrogant approach which is a definite mistake but is commonly seen in the world community of spiritual seekers. Practice has to be desired and enjoyed; it has to be attractive and compatible with your routines and responsibilities so that it is part of your lifestyle and not an addition to it. To bring this healthy relationship about however, you may need to realign old tendencies and this may mean some rigorous discipline in the beginning as new habits are given a chance to establish themselves. Depending on your conditioning this may take some time.

Be sincere and persist through obstacles, everybody has to wear down resistances. You are only human like everyone else. You will not get everything right, it will not always go smoothly, nature is just like that and as far as we know has always been like that. It is certainly like that for everyone around you and not just you. Aspire and proceed but be forgiving of yourself and understand that you are undertaking a way of living and being for the long term just like countless others have chosen to do throughout the ages. This choice is significant and highly legitimate; you can be delighted with it as the response to the calling you have always felt but have never quite satisfied. You are not alone, many others are with you and alongside you, the feelings you have are, within a yoga minority, common. There is no doubt that the current of guidance and the momentum that will propel and protect you is real. It is the basis for faith and trust and it has flowed in people like you for millennia.

The real is here and now

There is sometimes a tendency in yoga practitioners to deny the world and to adopt an unconscious assumption that practice is going to lead to a radically different and new set of perceptions. The ordinary and familiar world is shunned, dismissed or rebelled against. This assumption is fed and supported by endless spiritual texts which speak of visions, other dimensions and transcendental experiences. It gives the impression that awakening is not here and not of this world. This is not the case. Awakening is in the reality of this ordinary moment, within the observable norms that you are used to seeing and knowing. Of course spiritual events occur and when visionary experiences really speak to us, they are deeply and intensely profound, but they are not the purpose or the goal. The goal is in the deepening realisation and identification with the radiance of being at your very core. This is not in the unseen or the other dimensional. It is definitively here and now and in this ordinary experience of me, which of itself brightens and extends, within an I that you entirely recognise and know. It can be understood as the beautification of the moment.

Why do you need to look for another dimension? Isn't the one you are in now absolutely magnificent and full of all possibilities?

Atma Vichara is definitely not pushing away the world. It is a slow transformation at the very centre of your being while the world remains just as it is, and remember, it is tremendously beautiful and you are a key part of it. It has come upon you, you are meant to be here and to fulfil your destiny within it. Reality is here now, this is it, and it is marvellous and thrilling just as it is. Your calling and the response to that calling happens within this reality, not outside it.

Do not deny your circumstances. Your circumstances state the present moment, they are not wrong or unfair, they simply are, and awakening will emerge within them. Nature is far too complex for you to have it all your own way. Accept what is, flow with it, move with it, let choices express themselves right inside these circumstances and do not fantasise for another set of circumstances as if somehow what is happening now is a mistake. Be in the moment and witness the play of the moment as it evolves and stretches, full of variety, colour and life.

Perception remains, body remains, work and family remain, senses remain. What changes is identification from what you are not, to what you truly are. When this starts to happen, beauty is perceived everywhere and it is possible to see that denying the world and fighting against it is an impossible sham. Whatever arises is the reality, it is here and now, don't shut it out and deny it, don't push it away, that only leads to tension and hardship and is a mistake.

Don't think too much

There is no doubt at all that spiritual truth cannot be realised via intellect and logic. Of course theoretical explanations can give shape to things, but the assumption that realisation can come from the organising of concepts is deeply flawed. Truth is an experiential medium; it is direct and is in the felt centre, not in an abstract construct. The Upanishads say a very important thing about this:

Bright but hidden, the Self dwells in the heart.
Everything that moves, breathes, opens and closes lives in the Self.

He is the source of love and may be known through love but not through thought.

Mundaka Upanishad Part 2 v.1
(Easwaran page 113)

There is however, a strong tendency in yoga practitioners to unwittingly place their hopes in the territory of understanding it, getting on top of it, having it sorted out in their heads. To a degree that is necessary and essential because it is satisfying to feel secure and confident about something, to know the context within which practice arises, but this can only be a limited knowing. Resolution cannot be found here, as there will never be an end to intellectual searching. In fact it is counter-productive and sets up tensions as the hunt for understanding becomes fruitless. A philosophical construct is a useful foundation to practice because we need something to believe in, but do not try to understand it all, that is a barren road and will lead to getting tied up in frustrating intellectual circles.

The best approach to take is to study a few core texts, and recommendations are made in Annex 9. These are extremely high quality works, they are tested across time and you can put your faith in them with confidence. In this way texts link you to a tradition, they instil inspiration and security of approach, they encourage faith and motivation, they reveal increasing levels of meaning through repeated study as your own experience matures.

Resist the temptation to read anything or to keep searching for new angles and new answers. This is not empowering, it is confusing, it does not add, it depletes. Billions and billions of words are so easily and accessibly available these days that present perspective on the most esoteric, obscure and difficult concepts and practices. This is a modern phenomenon, as in previous ages, spiritual revelations were guarded and only accessed through effort after preliminary self-disciplines, by those who had proved themselves and earned it. Now anyone can get access to anything on a whim and with no grounding in either preparation, integrity or suitability. Such is the position of the time in which we try to manage the seeker's quest and apply effective sadhana.

It is a mistake to invest your energy in too much random research and information surfing which can easily become obsessive. See the study as the support but not the answer. Patient practice is the answer. What you want is only accessible through practice and direct encounter right in the centre of this moment, right in the immediate centre of you, in your feelings and experience and not in philosophy as an objective study. Avoid dilution, become a specialist, focus your study and exploration around a specialism, that is the way in which expertise and clarity of understanding develop, thereby encouraging and facilitating your practice. Atma Vichara and the core texts listed here which give the philosophical framework for it, represent such a specialism.

Why Atma Vichara is beneficial in life

What is the point of practising Atma Vichara? How does it help and why bother? These are legitimate questions to ask, especially amidst the diversity available to the seeker. There are five specific answers:

1. You are a spiritual seeker; there is something that you want. This urge is prompting you to do something about it to satisfy your yearning. The practice of Atma Vichara and the lifestyle context as it is being described here, provides you with a reliable, authentic and tested framework to do something about it. This is a powerful sadhana, an effective teaching that can bring trustworthy resolution to the seeker's search. For that reason it has a paramount benefit for all those to whom the above statement is meaningful, and particularly to those who have not found satisfaction from previous approaches.

2. Practice does not require special conditions; it is applicable by those to whom it appeals within any life cir-

cumstance. This is an important aspect, as once understood, and in the presence of the guidance and support described here, it ensures accessibility and equity. Renunciation or restricted conditions are not necessary.

3. As spiritual practice develops, altruistic qualities emerge; this is a natural consequence of the draw of the heart. This does not mean that we become morally or behaviourally perfect because the framework of our conditioned character will remain in place, but it does mean that we progressively become gentler, kinder and more tolerant people. That is a positive thing for the world.

4. As practice becomes more established, a range of other observable changes in outlook and thinking are likely to occur. These include:

   - A greater ease with daily life
   - Enhanced appreciation of beauty
   - Enhanced joy at the wonder of nature in all its parts
   - Absence of fear or great courage in the face of it
   - Spontaneity and freedom of action
   - Abundant energy
   - Endurance and strength when it is required
   - Creativity and productivity
   - Confident security
   - Effortless non-attachment
   - Experiencing Self as enduring love and presence

These things are life-enhancing, they are descriptors of happiness and they are qualities which oil the flow of daily life. They benefit you and the people around you.

5. As practice deepens, the promised effects of pursuing the practice are:

   The end of the sense of separateness
   Absorption in the heart
   Effortless freedom

These things are profound and beautiful, they are what you seek and can be described as self-realisation. For that reason this sadhana is highly relevant and the refuge for mature seekers.

Commentary on lifestyle

Live well in enjoyment, productivity and easy relationship

Spiritual life has never been easy due to the vagaries and dominance of the mind and the pull and push of our conditioned nature. Yet all around the world and across time, people do apply themselves seriously to spiritual life. The fact that it is often hard need not disturb us or limit us. It seems that all processes of birth and growth involve a struggle, a mixture of both delight and discomfort. But you do not really have a choice in this. The calling of the heart is asserting itself and destiny is unfolding. For those who are reading this book with eagerness, awakening will not be a peripheral interest; it will be the central theme of life or at least a strong fascination. This needs to be recognised and facilitated. It needs to be enabled and addressed, but what is the lifestyle which will achieve this? What preparation or alteration is required?

Renunciation

Solitude is in the mind
One might be in the thick of the world and maintain serenity
of mind
Such a one is in solitude
Another may stay in a forest, but still be unable to control his
mind
He cannot be said to be in solitude
Solitude is a function of mind not of place
A man attached to desire cannot get solitude wherever he
may be
A detached man is always in solitude
                    Sri Ramana Maharshi   Talks-20

A strong tradition in spiritual life is to renounce the world and retreat, so that contemplation and devotion can be practised in solitude away from distraction. Although this remains a valid choice and may at times be relevant, it cannot be the only choice. For a spiritual practice to be truly direct and authentic it must be accessible to all and in all circumstances. We need a model for our time which enables all people, family people, working people, single people, and retired people to satisfy the calling and yearning in the heart and to undertake a comprehensive lifelong sadhana within the rigour of daily life and whatever ordinary circumstances unfold. Without question, Atma Vichara offers this opportunity. Once understood, it can be applied in any circumstances because it is based on this premise:

Action is flowing through you automatically, as an expression of conditioning. You are not these actions; neither are you the doer of these actions. You are the presence of being within which all actions arise and within which they flow. This presence of being is without break, it truly is the enduring present; it is never not going to be there, unlike the actions which will all rise, change and die.

It is not necessary to renounce circumstance nor retreat from circumstance. Whilst respite can be nourishing and productive, ordinary outward life must be allowed to unfold naturally. Whilst that continues to happen, we can increasingly experience the freedom and non-attachment to circumstance that comes through abiding as the enduring presence and allowing the actions to take care of themselves. This does not imply passivity or lack of responsibility, for action, choice and outcome will continue to rise as the moment unfolds. The forces of discrimination and intelligence assert their influence and direct the application of the moment. It is not you who puts the effort into driving this, because you are not the personal doer of actions, doing just happens; including the assertion of whatever is needed in reaction to events.

Practice and work

Your work is action and service. It is a function of the society within which this body was born. It is your duty – your *dharma* to work and serve. Whatever your responsibilities may be let the productivity you have within your capabilities as a human being express well as positive service through work.

The world of modern work is, however, tremendously busy, complex and demanding. When you are in the midst of activity and responsibilities, endeavour, interactivity and movement is flowing. The mind is engaged, action and reaction are dominant. In the context of easy and attractive work, this will be pleasant and will result in the feeling of satisfaction and reward; in the context of demanding, complex or tedious work, this will lead to the feeling of strain and pressure. These outcomes are largely inevitable and can't be denied. Everybody's working life will be characterised by rewarding successes and difficult demands. One of the greatest mistakes in yoga is to try and resist this by attempting to enforce calmness and harmony in all situations, or to expect perpetual ease in your work. Nature is not like this and to try and make it so will only produce anxiety and tension. When there is calmness enjoy it, when there is ferocious activity watch yourself engage with it and allow your actions to respond as a warrior *yogi*. Once again what comes, comes, including your choices and reactions, it is nature. To try and force against the tide is incompatible with nature and foolish. There is nothing wrong with seeking pleasant work that suits your skills and abilities, that is simply efficient, but don't let it become an escape or a limitation. Engagement, adaptability and flexibility is the way. The very development of practice will of its own accord, change the attitude and capabilities to work, and enable you to realise that you are truly not the doer, but this appreciation cannot be forced or pushed. The approach to take to everyday work and responsibilities is this:

- When in activity let it come, accept it, attention will flow into the activity and will engage with it. When this happens you are bound to feel more personalised, more of the body, more in the driving seat. The mind will be active and working.

- In the spaces between activity, and when leisure moments are available, easy attention is brought to practice where beingness prevails. Then increasingly the mind is at rest and not working.

- Through time and through taking the above approach, the strength of your current increases, enabling you to leave the doer to do its tasks spontaneously, whatever the demand; in the secure and obvious recognition that the doer and the beautiful creativity of the doing are automatic, boundless and taking care of themselves.

The greatest barrier to integrating work is the sense that there is someone to defend, sensibilities to promote, something to prove or needs to assert. Attitudes of mind that drive us to be either too controlling or a perfectionist, to be defensive, to always want to be liked and approved of, to need to have everything completed, to always expect clarity, order and an absence of problems etc etc are some of the key reasons for stress and difficulty in work. When, through practice, these assertions weaken, because they are seen as habits and constraining memories of conditioning, tremendous freedoms of capability and durability are released. In the same way that you are being lived you are also being worked. You can trust nature to take care of it and can submit to the flow of it. In this way you can learn to enjoy it, be fascinated by it and not deny it. Such a positive approach towards work emerges through practice and is a beautiful, liberating force in life.

There is no doubt however, that in the material sense, work, especially for sensitive people (which many seekers are) can be taxing. We must allow the worker to work but also pay attention to her need for rest and care. The approach of harsh austerity has definitely been shown to be destructive. Be productive but take it as easy as circumstances allow. Do anything you can, practically within your work environment and personal arrangements, to protect and nurture yourself. Be honest about your capabilities, ask for help when needed, don't struggle alone and take rest where you can. Work hard by all means, be disciplined and adventurous by all means, but take pleasure and comfort in equal measure. Within the context of discrimination and social norms be as you are not as you would like to appear.

Action

The person must act, action is good, it is seeded in nature and is infinitely dynamic. Activity, work, life events and the flow of appearance are fascinating. Despite tribulations we should be grateful for the opportunity to witness this participation and experience this vibrant variety and creativity, grateful for this abundant experience of life.

However this does not mean that everything is always good, nice or even safe. Infinite forces are at work in the world, both positive and negative, both harmless and harmful, both selfless and selfish. Throughout recorded history it has been like this and is likely to continue to be so. It must be accepted that however we may or may not approve, this is the way nature currently is. Most are acting for good and in consideration of others, but not all. The perspectives people hold are complicated, a great deal of need and desire is felt in the infinity of minds, which expresses either consciously or unconsciously through powerful and largely unstoppable behaviours. The facts and events of our own lives are also largely unpredictable and neutral, in the sense that things may happen that you don't perceive as fair, or even just, but nature is like this – neutral. It is not acting on your terms. It is not adhering to your wishes and wants. Unless of course your wishes and wants are themselves aligned to what is.

If you stand on the beach, whether you like it or not, the ocean is coming in, it will either wash you clean or drown you depending on how you act. Now you may have views about that, but the ocean will not, it is just being the ocean, no matter how you may plead with it to change. You could of course prevent the ocean coming on to the beach, but this would involve huge industrial construction to complete a suitable barrier. Even if you did that, you would have to build the barrier on the ocean's terms and not on yours. It is better to enjoy the beach at low tide and choose to move up it when the tide comes in.

Relationship with life is like this. It is all coming in the only way it can, in that moment. You may perceive it as good or bad and react accordingly, but in reality it is just stating in that moment, the only possible implementation of what the past has led to. Adversity and difficulties are bound to arise but we should not be afraid of them. Enduring challenge, and not rushing to escape it, develops strength, and strength is an extremely valuable if not essential component in spiritual life. Your actions are coming, they cannot be denied but they can be influenced, shaped and crucially orientated towards the good, the positive, the compassionate and the just.

Ethics

Clearly people make choices although, as we have previously discussed, the process of choice making is itself largely automatic i.e. the outcome chosen is bound to be. It does not feel this way, it feels purposeful and optional as the commentary of decision-making weaves its way this way and that. Either assertively or passively, choices are bound to arise in everybody. All spiritual traditions throughout the world advise a moral and ethical code upon which the ideals of choice can be based. When you look at these differing sets of guidance they illustrate a common theme, which is selfless, compassionate action, delivered in strength, self-control and love. They advise respect for others, consideration and avoiding harm where possible.

Perhaps Jesus best summarised all these themes in his ground-breaking statement:

"Love your neighbour as yourself."

Patanjali contributes to this with a similarly ground-breaking statement:

"Do no harm."

A primary statement from the Buddha is:

"Be compassionate."

For yoga people the set of objectives that describe how to observe and conduct life are the *yamas* and *niyamas* coordinated within the Yoga Sutras. They speak of tolerance, modesty, acceptance, contentment and kindness.

They are:

Ahimsa	Act with non-violence
Satya	Apply truthfulness
Asteya	Do not wrongly take from others
Brahmacharya	Be moderate in passion and energy
Aparigrara	Do not expect more than you need
Shauca	Seek cleanliness and purity in all
Samtosha	Be contented with what is
Tapas	Apply spiritual practice
Svadhyaya	Study the truth
Ishvarapranidhanani	Surrender to the inner power

Further detail and commentary on these aspects of ethical behaviour are easily available within the yoga literature for those who are not familiar with them.

None of these codes of conduct have been deliberately worked out as a set of austerities. They are statements of how behaviour naturally arranges itself when the spirit is realised and the heart is open. Within the presence of strength we should all aim to devote our energies to the promotion of the positive, the compassionate, the tolerant and the productive, to collaborate with the beauty of nature and to do good. We should all aim to confidently release this power to do good within us and to turn away from the destructive, the negative, the intolerant and the harmful. This is collaborative living as a citizen of the world.

However, the world is complex and you too are complex, the nuances of good and bad, right and wrong are intricate, within the context of numerous pressures, duties, wants and needs. Far too much strife and denial is caused in trying to force good thoughts and good actions and in assigning judgement, leading to guilt, uncertainty and blame. Aspiration to be selfless is good, personal discipline is good, but denying and suppressing natural expression (or attempting to) leads to tension, frustration and disappointment. Balance, tolerance and acceptance towards yourself, alongside sensitivity towards others, is called for, personal forgiveness is called for.

Be as you are

Atma Vichara takes such a stance. Within the boundaries of the ethical position discussed above, be as you are without trying to force what you are not. Allow action to flow and invest all your energy in realising to whom the action appears. Once the current of the heart responds and the presence of being makes itself felt, behaviours will re-arrange themselves automatically because the natural status of the heart is to pacify the mind, to promote peace, acceptance and love, in the presence of strength and courageous discrimination.

There is a reason for this; yoga teaches us that all drives and wants are prompted by the *vasanas* that seed the subconscious through successive lives, sometimes leading to compulsion, dominance and selfishness. The practice of

Atma Vichara that leads to abidance in the heart erodes and dissolves these vasanas as the following dialogue highlights:

Questioner:
Distractions result from inherited tendencies (vasanas). Can they be cast off?

"Yes they are certainly obliterated and many have done so because they believed they could. It is done by concentration on that which is free from vasanas and yet is their core."
Sri Ramana Maharshi talks-28

"As the meditation on the Self rises higher and higher vasanas will be destroyed."
Sri Ramana Maharshi Nan Yar-13

Please just notice for a moment the huge importance of that statement. It really is immense; perhaps Christians may term it the forgiveness of God. It means that the very process of the rising of the heart's properties which Atma Vichara creates, that very process, burns off the vasanas, causing a fading of their characteristics and a quietening of the desires and habits which otherwise burden and direct us.

Personality

The practice of Atma Vichara will lead to an overarching change, a softening and a gentleness of spirit as indicated above, but even then, everyone has their own personality through which characteristics manifest, which is observable throughout life. Your habits may change, your behaviours and interests may re-arrange, but to observers you will still be recognisable as the same you. Fundamental lines of character endure, they are archetypal seeds within your genes and should not, in fact, cannot be denied, they are in your very cells reinforced and structured through your upbringing, culture and social circumstance. You may be a strong and dynamic leader, you may be a passive follower, you may be dominant or timid, adventurous or cautious, you may be gregarious and sociable or quiet and private, you may be uninhibited and expressive or you may be shy, a rebel, or a conformist, you may be capable of great endurance or not, or any combination of the above. These fundamental characteristics are what this body and mind have temporarily become. This does not mean a person cannot change, for clearly a person can and will change as maturity and experience moulds us, but certain aspects of the you that was born as you will manifest, show themselves and catch your attention throughout life. It is helpful to accept this, so that you are not fighting or denying something which could otherwise easily be assimilated and happily lived with. Within the context of *ahimsa* all characteristics can be accepted as the framework within which this body expresses and acts. Just as all nature is rich in variety, so are you and those around you. Realising this leads to a very important rule regarding your own self-importance.

Self-importance

You are unique and important but you are not more important than anyone else. Everyone is different, everyone is trying to respond to the forces that drive them and everyone has a right to be who they are. Sometimes you will like what you see and sometimes you will not, and you will take action appropriately as best you can, but you are not the judging centre that can define exactly what should or should not be. The world is infinitely varied and is not operating or conforming to your design and neither should it. Following your destiny is important and inevitable but is not any more important than the destiny of others.

Try to see the differences in people as beautiful and creative, for indeed they are. The choice you have taken to respond to the spiritual calling within you is fabulous and wonderful, the choices other people make and the actions that shape them are also valid and a part of the whole. It is best to be responsible and alert, true to yourself, decisive in your action and reaction to what comes but fundamentally not judgemental.

The best approach is to see the wonder and creativity in all things and enjoy the beauty the world has to offer, aspire for goodness, and accept yourself without guilt, you are only human and you have not consciously chosen the parameters within which your humanity expresses itself, neither has anyone else. In that sense we are all in it together, and that gives us all a common bond and a common opportunity to support and nourish one another where we can.

Be ordinary

One of the great misapprehensions in the yoga community is the feeling you are special and the striving to be so. In a way we are special, but only because the wondrous creativity of nature is in itself special and that can be seen in everybody not just us. It is of course true that we pursue a minority interest and choose a medium for its expression which is not of western culture, but these distinctions are increasingly irrelevant in this global village, which states the culture of the modern world. This minority interest though, is itself only an expression of the common desire for happiness, contentment, meaning and love and there are many minority interests that may claim the same purpose. A small number of people take to yoga; an even smaller group take to yoga as a serious spiritual path and of those, only a few will truly and sincerely embrace Atma Vichara. In that sense we are a minority and it is only that fact which makes us special. People seek attainment in different ways: through physical accomplishment, intellectual accomplishment, practical accomplishment and the acquiring of numerous skills. You have chosen spiritual accomplishment and you are glad of it because it seems to be the foundation upon which all else is based, but that is just the way you see it, that is where your destiny has brought you, other destinies travel in different directions which could be argued to be equally valid. The point of seeing it like this is not to put yourself on a pedestal in comparison with others. You are following a sincere and committed personal discipline, your heart's calling. That is fantastic, it will define your life but it is not the way everybody else must also be.

Similarly great rivalries can occur amongst differing yoga traditions, religions and philosophies. Steer clear of all these judgements and destructive critiques. There is no harm in comparison because this aids learning, but competing with or decrying another system is foolish. When we can see openly the heart of all religions, we simply see commonality, when we can be open to the sincerity of people who may be following radically different systems; we simply see spiritual brothers and sisters. There is a common centre and a common intent in the energetic principles within the Christian cathedral, the Hindu temple, the Buddhist temple and the Yoga sadhana hall. Because people are different, the language of understanding, communication and practice is different but the central theme and the calling in the heart is definitely the same across all mystic gatherings and communities.

See it like this, see the diversity as marvellous and thrilling, see it as evidence of the validity of pursuing a spiritual calling, it is not just happening to you, it is happening to many and will continue to happen. Your only duty is to respond, to be clear about your own sadhana and to proceed as a spiritual citizen of the world community and the yoga fellowship.

This approach of ordinariness applies also to lifestyle. As we mature through yoga we gather about us various accoutrements, attitudes and habits. Our bookshelves swell and our collections of beads, crystals, bells and pictures etc expands. In a way this is all a joke but clearly there is nothing wrong with humour and fun along the way; it is one of the delights of life. We may all entertain ourselves with the ornaments of spiritual practice that come to us but don't be too precious about it, remember you are not special you are just pursuing a special interest that has certain traditions behind it. Embrace them by all means, but also be ordinary and live an ordinary life. All the common structures of relationship, family, work, leisure, economics and modern lifestyle are entirely compatible with a spiritual life. Indeed that is the very fabric of nature within which we find ourselves. So that must be our starting point and our place of continuation.

And what a splendid place it is, or through this practice can be seen to be. Simply acknowledging that and enjoying that is an important milestone. A key and delightful way to bring this about is to be in the natural world and really appreciate what's around you.

Walk in nature

Spending time in nature is not only pleasant, it is important for the seeker. There is a healing refreshment that flourishes by engaging with natural wonder. This acts as a balance to our other exertions and responsibilities especially if we spend a lot of time in towns, streets and offices. Walking in gardens, parks and amongst trees, cycling down country lanes, lying in the fields, feeding the birds, climbing the hills, soothe and inspire, and these are qualities that facilitate the opening to the spirit. How glorious this world is, how beautiful the spring, the summer, the autumn and the winter. How clean open air feeds us, how the ocean surf cleanses us, how the sun, the wind, the rain and the mountains change our mood and free the spirit.

Spend time in nature, in wild places and in landscaped places, linger in gardens and seek out wilderness. Get to know fields, flowers, trees and the smell of the wind. Engage with them, gaze upon them, walk amongst them regularly, feel yourself to be touched by them, part of them. Sense and touch the open spaces and the natural beauty of life and sky and earth and growth.

Difficulties encountered in sadhana

Despite intense moments from time to time, all is well

The commentary already outlined, gives extensive guidance on the application of sadhana in life. It will also be useful for some to have more detail on specific issues relating to energy that can sometimes arise in sadhana. This is not applicable for all and is not an inevitable consequence of practice but it will be highly relevant for some. Everything depends on karma, the course of your sadhana like the course of your life, is a reflection of the conditioning within the body and mind that you are temporarily associated with. The Mundaka Upanishad gives a beautiful description of this association:

Like two golden birds perched on the self-same tree, intimate friends, the ego and the Self dwell in the same body. The former eats the sweet and sour fruits of the tree of life while the latter looks on in detachment.

Mundaka Upanishad Part 3 v.1
(Easwaran page 115)

The eating of the sweet and sour fruit describes active life. Part of your active life is sadhana. If you read the spiritual literature of any tradition you see common reports of energetic events which people experience. These are described in various ways as mystical, psychological, psychic or divine. Many accounts are given from radically different cultures and times regarding religious experience, visions, insights, intuition, poetry, art, etc. In just the same way it is easily observable in the yoga community that some people are affected dynamically by their practice. The term *kundalini* is the yoga term most often used to depict this. It is descriptive of the transformative power of inspiration, expression and change in nature. For almost all, this is a benefit rather than a problem or a burden; it brings added dimensions to life and only requires assimilation and some sensible management. This is of course also true in the normal run of events, as any excitability, strong passion or keen desire brings both problems and benefits that require respect and care. In this sense it is a normal extension to life's experience and can be considered as such.

Specific interpretations for different individuals can vary a great deal but in the following paragraphs five primary themes are described. The aim is to reassure those who experience these things and to offer advice regarding simple approaches to management. More personalised and specific commentary is the province of the student/teacher relationship.

The turbulent mind

A common phenomenon in spiritual life is that the process of change often produces an upsurge of critical thoughts, strong desires and selfish ideas; the very mind which we hope to pacify seems to react, surge and present its worst (those instincts, perspectives and thoughts we would rather deny). This experience is well recognised and considered to be a likely, but not inevitable, element of transformation.

As discussed, the subconscious is constructed on the vasanas that shape our conditioning; often they are deeply buried and unrecognised but are either driving our thinking or limiting our willingness to explore the new. Transcending the ego does not happen overnight so that we are suddenly never troubled by an unwelcome thought again, transcending the ego happens through the progressive non-identification with the ego's very structure and its associated wants and needs. In this reorientation reactions may well occur in the mind. This is really not surprising as the energy of dynamic change is alive and acting. What does change mean? It means embracing, integrating and allowing the different; it means the shedding of the old. Anyone who has ever moved from a place of familiarity and routine to a place unknown and untested will know that this is an adventurous thing to do. It brings challenge, the exposure of weaknesses, the familiarising of new experiences and some disorientation or upheaval. It is the same here. You cannot have what you want yet remain as you are.

All kinds of thoughts arise in meditation, it is but right. What lies hidden in you is brought out. Unless they rise up how can they be destroyed? They rise up spontaneously in order to be extinguished in due course.

Sri Ramana Maharshi Talks- 310

When we are led into any dynamic change, there is a certain force behind it, a momentum which carries us along. In committed spiritual life, experience has shown that when the interest to seek the truth is awake in a person, then the process is already underway. It is not a process that can be shaped or contained by the will; clearly, in taking account of all that has been said so far, that would be ridiculous.

The approach then is to allow yourself to be changed, not through being in charge, not through the approval of the commentating mind but through openness, receptivity and non-resistance. The qualities required are faith, patience, bravery, trust and relaxed endurance. The assistance required is support and guidance. The key thing is to not try to push these thoughts away nor deny them, instead allow them but do not indulge them or follow them with your interest. These thoughts are temporary and insubstantial appearing like background music. See beyond them by identifying as the presence of being within which they arise.

When unwelcome thoughts appear in the context of sadhana, key features of advice are:

- Understand it to be normal and common
- Have faith that it is temporary and will not overwhelm you
- Don't act on the thoughts, this in itself undermines them

- Keep going with your practice
- Remain vigilant in asking to whom are the thoughts arising
- Keep close association with sangha and *satsang*

Depending on your particular conditioning, you may need to take this approach for some time, but this can easily be done and has been the recognised way across traditions and across time. It's not just happening to you, it almost certainly will not get out of control, it's not your fault, you are not a bad person, you are just human like everybody else.

In this sense and perhaps ironically, the chaotic mind, when in the context of sadhana, is considered good as it is a symptom of change. To some degree there may always be elements of distracting thoughts, but they will increasingly recede into the background and are of no consequence because you do not give them your interest or invest meaning in them. They are no more than chatter and noise being witnessed then ignored.

Shakti

Shakti is the Sanskrit term for energy or force. Shakti is evident everywhere in the motion of all things. One of the effects of a deep yoga practice can sometimes be the gradual or sudden appearance of increased shakti within us. This does not happen to everyone but it does happen to some. It is a real power, it is not something imagined. Whilst being a wonderful thing leading to creative productivity, enthusiasm, liveliness and strength, it can also have a keen downside, namely becoming over-stimulated and over-alert. The source from which this power comes is truly amazing and a very interesting thing to experience. Energy appears in abundant quantities, it is as if a generator has been switched on, it can in fact feel like a hum, a glow or a light constant pressure. When fully integrated, this shakti is a tremendously valuable and welcome thing. It is a transforming power, automatically fuelling spiritual practice and indeed all other activity. It is the power in the machine and is well recognised in yoga. In many ways this power takes over and directs change but its acceleration can be intense. Prior to integration this intensity can be disruptive and tiresome. Being over-stimulated means it is difficult to sleep or truly relax, becoming restless, driven or anxious is a real possibility. This can wear us out and we experience a hyper-alert yet jet-lagged condition which can make practical life hard to cope with. If this happens it is, in the context of our sadhana, normal. Nothing has gone wrong and there is nothing to be afraid of, it happens to some seekers, for those people it can be said to be part of nature's process and a necessary force of transformation and change. It needs to be lived through and not fought against. In time it will integrate of itself as a new energy in you, which will be very welcome and will become a familiar part of your life. Until this occurs the approach to take is one of patient acceptance, whilst respecting and self-managing things in the following way:

- Don't overdo it, avoid over excitement (however tempting)
- Watch your diet, this definitely has a big influence
- Put your energy into an appealing creative project of some kind
- Take moderate physical exercise regularly
- Take suitable rest regularly
- Manage your domestic routine to facilitate sleep
- Take a break from reading esoteric subjects
- For those practising *hatha* yoga use light *asana* and *nadi shodhana* only
- Practise simple *yoga nidra*
- Spend time with your teacher
- Spend time in close association with sangha
- Be in nature often
- Avoid being over serious, try to stay happy and playful

For most there is no need to alter common routines, work,

interests and family life can continue, but some cutting back of activity and taking sensible respites will be helpful. The key and essential thing to know is that it is natural, normal and alright. Change is always dynamic, by being patient and taking the above advice into account, you will easily learn to assimilate this force, not because you have tamed it or worked anything out, but because its very presence has of itself integrated into you. As this occurs you will come to see this particular shakti as a great gift and a most welcome friend.

Sensitivity

Another potential difficulty for spiritual practitioners is expanded sensitivity. Suddenly, or as a gradual development, we can become tremendously open. This is a good thing but means we are potentially more vulnerable. We can be easily hurt, emotionally reactive, susceptible to atmospheres (either real or imagined) and liable to shock, especially in the presence of anger, threat or criticism. There is a real need for security and we crave tenderness, gentleness and positive affirmation.

The upside of sensitivity, and it is a huge upside, is that love, joy and delight are heightened. Honesty, truthfulness and sincerity declare themselves as your very nature and the potential to appreciate beauty is hugely multiplied. Nonetheless the world and the society in which we live and work does not necessarily accommodate sensitivity easily or even welcome it. A certain ability to discriminate and protect ourselves from negative influences is helpful to assimilate.

The approach to adopt is this:

- Don't take yourself too seriously, you are less important than you think
- Don't try to over-analyse or understand everything's meaning

- Try to minimise exposure to harsh company and negative stimulus
- Ground yourself in ordinary work and domestic activity
- See fellowship in sangha as very important
- Be brave and accept temporary upset, as temporary
- Don't expect others to be as sensitive as you or to treat you sensitively
- If physical sensitivities affect you, access natural remedies in response

The key to living with sensitivity is to accept it as part of you and enjoy it, but not take too much interest in it. It just is. Leave it and the body-mind, within which it appears, to take care of itself. Sometimes sensitivity leads to perceptual experiences, inner sights, sounds, feelings etc which, if they occur may well affect us profoundly. React of course but again do not over- analyse or invest too much importance in it. Let the natural discrimination that develops through experience and maturity integrate these things and look after you. Whatever needs to happen will happen. Learn to avoid the mental commentary referred to earlier, learn to be in the moment fully and not in the analysis of the past or the projection of the future. There really is no one and nothing to defend, there is nothing to fix or make better, nothing to protect or project. There is just the beautiful presence of the unfolding moment and reaction appearing in it. If that reaction is occasionally experienced as vulnerability or shock, that is alright. It will pass, you do not need to dwell in it, let the new moment be new and move on with it.

Big ideas

Keep things ordinary, because even the ordinary is truly extraordinary. As has already been explained, for most, pursuing this practice whilst remaining within existing circumstances is the correct approach. It is important to know this because sometimes big new ideas present themselves and become very fascinating or compelling.

Giving everything up to go and live in a Himalayan hermitage, abandoning our career, moving into a religious community, leaving our family, giving away our possessions, selling our car because we feel suddenly guilty about pollution, deciding to become an artist when we have absolutely no talent for art, etc. All these things result from excitement, the yearning for change and the desire for satisfaction. They are symptomatic of transformation, of the quest for purity and love.

Clearly, inspiration and motivation is a great thing and suppression is usually non-productive. Where something needs to happen, it will definitely happen, even if it is radical. If you truly need to become a hermit that will happen, if your relationship is unfruitful and changing it is in your destiny, it will be unstoppable but in the main, where sudden compelling big ideas appear, they should be given time and allowed to mature before acting on them. It can often be a temporary symptom of openness and expanded energy rather than a definitive life direction. Living and evolving through your ordinary circumstances is the best way for most. The practice of Atma Vichara will enable you to see the beauty and potential of where you are and to learn how to get the best from that, rather than chasing shadows. Unless of course shadows are simply the shape of the new, appearing dimly.

Supporting relationships

Although you may be very inspired, not everyone else is, or is necessarily that interested. Despite a tendency to want to encourage inspiration in those around you, that is not necessarily the right thing to do. Whatever our close relationships are, behavioural changes in you are keenly noticed in others, obviously affect others and vice versa. Find the right way for your particular situation to share thoughts and feelings so that your partner, your family and your close associates recognise what's important to you. However they do not have to agree with you, you do not have to make them feel the same way as you, you do not have to change their ideas. Where that is going to happen it will happen anyway. You may be in a relationship where all parties are equally motivated and if that is so then fine, but it is an observable fact in the yoga community, that relationships are more commonly created with one partner being strongly spiritually motivated towards sadhana and the other not so, or differently so. Again this is not unusual in life; often special interests are not fully shared. On occasions this may frustrate or sadden you but unless your interests are being destructively criticised then do not see this arrangement as necessarily wrong. It seems that there is some property in nature that brings us together in this way.

Mutual supportive respect for one another is what needs to be achieved and if you can bring that about then that is enough. Often sadhana is a private thing, not a secret thing, but a discreet thing, quietly applied within ordinary circumstances. Where things are important to you, where you are experiencing thoughts, ideas or insights of course it is right to share them with your loved ones, but you intuitively know what the right level and the right style of this sharing is. Be happy with that and don't try to convert or enforce what's clear to you on others unless it is invited. Also remember that your behaviour and conviction can be challenging to live with itself from time to time. This is another reason why satsang and *sangham* is so essential for spiritual practitioners, for in that relationship you can let yourself go totally, have sharing with others and be yourself. For many that is where fulfilment and support can be most appropriately sought.

Sangham
The Support of
Community

SANGHAM
The support of community

The four refuges

Take refuge in the happy fellowship of like-minded sisters and brothers

Applying ourselves to sadhana within the context of ordinary life is a great destiny and privilege. It is not a path open to everybody but it is a path unavoidable for some. Those people must themselves recognise that treading this path requires skill and energy. The good news is that this is well understood in the yoga tradition which has a clear perspective on how support should be sought and provided. The formulae that best expresses this are the four refuges that were included in the introduction and have been expressed in the structure of the previous chapters. It is the fellowship and community of sangha that has underpinned the seeker's life for millennia and has provided the support and belonging, that keeps faith, effort and awakening alive. Sangha is the fourth refuge and can only be understood within the context of the other three. Let us consider this profound and life-changing structure again and the satsang that is available from it before speaking once more of community:

- Satyam Sharanam Gachami
  I take refuge in the truth

- Yogam Sharanam Gachami
  I take refuge in yoga

- Guram Sharanam Gachami
  I take refuge in the guru

- Sangham Sharanam Gachami
  I take refuge in the community of practitioners

Satyam and yogam

The truth exists but it is not theoretical, it is experiential. It is not a piece of understanding or a conclusion in intellect. Truth is the direct arising of self-realisation in the very felt centre of our own being. No one else can give this to you; neither can it be acquired indirectly. It can only be seen or realised through the insight that comes from personal awakening. The only route towards this is the intimate endeavour of applied practice (sadhana). You have to be practising; you have to have an interest and an attraction for it. You have to be building it into the everyday construction of your life so that it is a cosy and familiar friend, a constant part of your habits and priorities. This does not need to be lonely or isolated; in fact it is essential that it isn't. Your practice needs the potent influence of a teacher, the rich nourishment of satsang and the encouragement of sangha.

Guram

The term *guru* refers to the presence in the world of teaching and teachers. It refers to the force of incisive transmission and influence that can dispel ignorance and engender the dynamic alignment of interest and vision in an individual that awakens change. This is best described as a current, it is not reliant on personality but on the inner and spontaneous resources of the teacher and the receptivity of the pupil. It is a mysterious thing and largely unconscious. Although it is often characterised by a relationship of love, closeness, and respect often it will provoke challenge. Whatever the impact, having access to a teacher provides deep security and comfort; it represents a point of reference on which the seeker can draw either directly or virtually.

For some people the teacher is no longer living but the sense of potent relationship is unaffected by this, for others the teacher is only accessed periodically and often rarely, yet the fact the teacher exists is enough. For others the relationship is close, frequent and familiar, there is no absolute model but there is the recognition that having someone you refer to as guru or teacher is of immense value.

The current through which the guru acts is of course all one power and from the same source. Whilst the personification of teachers remains the chosen preference for many, as it offers a living and dynamic mouthpiece through which we can interact, in effect the essential guru is the Self and is the calling we feel from within.

Sri Nisargadatta summed it up perfectly when he said:

"Your own Self is your ultimate teacher
The outer teacher is merely a milestone
It is only your inner teacher that will walk with you to the
goal
For he is the goal."
                    Sri Nisargadatta Maharaj in "I Am That"

Nonetheless as you will keenly know, milestones can be a welcome and often essential aid in any journey to clarify position and direction. Teachers should be accessed, valued and supported for this reason. Satsang should be sought.

Satsang

Satsang is very ancient, it means being in the company of the wise. It is a chance to be with a teacher and imbibe the dynamic qualities that that relationship offers. This is not a conscious thing, it is a vital thing. Time and again it is observable that the teaching that emerges in satsang commonly goes right to the heart of the matter for those in the company who have a great need, again this is unspoken, there is something in the nature of it, something intuitive, something unconscious that, dependent on the teacher's maturity, moves as the current of yoga.

Satsang has a common arrangement, people gather, there is

a relaxed and dynamic atmosphere, either silence prevails or talking begins which often but not always leads to question, answer and common discussion. This is very upanishadic and authentic and can be evidenced throughout history. It states the direct tradition of live teaching, of sitting down with the teacher, of imbibing the guru force. This means the articulation through speech or silence of the current of influence by which we, like those before and after us, are shown the light. There is something truly timeless and majestic in this. It is of great value and great beauty. Satsang may not always go well (although it mostly does), it may not always be what you want to hear, but it is the place where doubts are raised and doubts are cleared.

Sangham

Throughout history people have grouped themselves around communities to support their spiritual practice; this is fundamental in the yoga tradition but can also be observed in all other traditions across the globe. It is well recognised that for those with a sincere interest in spiritual development, having a link with others of similar interests and inclinations is immensely valuable and probably essential. As we have said earlier you are pursuing a minority interest, which the lifestyle of the majority does not facilitate and which the set-up of society and that which drives it, in the main, does not support. As practical people we have to fit within this context, to be of the world and in the world but free of the world all at the same time. Common forces of economics, health, politics, crime, risks and hazards, media and education impact upon us all. The added dimension for you is that within and amongst this you are pursuing a committed spiritual life.

This is the way for the modern yogi, belonging to and participating in a community of like-minded or like-intentioned people is a key foundation by which spiritual life is sustained and supported. In Sanskrit we call this community sangha. Being with others where you can be yourself, you can discuss ideas, you can share doubts, you can offer encouragement and receive encouragement, you can experience friendship, you can be open and not criticised in an uninformed way for your openness. You can be nourished by the recognition that you are not alone and where you can be strengthened and feel part of a whole. All these things are the product of sangha, they are beautiful and dynamic. Sangha is a node through which the current of yoga flows. It is a key foundation of practice.

Community ashram life

Throughout the yoga tradition sangha has often constructed or centred itself around the focus of an *ashram*, a physical place of belonging and communal living. Ashram has been the commitment and the structure within which communal spiritual life has been lived. The aspects of this ashram life by which the yoga tradition has been kept alive are well-founded and tested. They can be described as:

- The presence of a teacher and teachings
- Opportunity for satsang and sincere committed sadhana
- Living as part of a community of practitioners
- Opportunity to work as *seva* on behalf of the ashram

Ashrams have traditionally been communal centres in single locations, often separate from ordinary life, set up as retreats within which spiritual practice is pursued through a monastic style of life. While these remain as important resources which can be accessed for nourishment and respite, we need an additional model for the modern age which is not dependent on renunciation. A model which enables individuals to work and live a mainstream life but still pursue a committed yoga path.

Such a model can be developed through the establishment of a community ashram. This acknowledges that fulfilling ashram criteria does not need a physical building, a residential centre or a protected way of life. The aspects of ashram life can instead be replicated in a set of arrangements that enable individuals to maintain ordinary and family responsibilities but still follow a profound inner calling; facilitated and supported by regular contact, satsang and a common shared purpose. The elements that describe this set of arrangements are:

- A clear, mature and tested core teaching
- A lineage or tradition in which that teaching is grounded

- A teacher to act as spiritual director and living focal point of the teaching
- A fellowship of people committed to the teaching
- Regular meetings which enable access to satsang and sadhana
- Opportunities for concentrated personal practice
- Teaching resources that support and facilitate deepening sadhana
- Opportunities to practice *karma yoga* through service to the ashram
- Productivity in the world through work and engagement with life

The Yogaliving community ashram, by whom this book has been published, is an evolution in implementing these arrangements. It is making available opportunities, amidst everyday society and independent lifestyles, by which individuals can have a sense of belonging and a structure to support sangha and the practice of Atma Vichara in the modern world.

Summary
Of
Approach

Summary of Approach
The conclusion of sadhana

*Let conviction, clarity and confidence show the way
to action*

There is nothing to do except to be still, attentive and alert. In this stillness there is something present. Realising and recognising that presence of being, surrendering all attention into the openness of that is what the sadhana of Atma Vichara is for.

In any moment endless activity is taking place. The day is full of variety. Thoughts and ideas, sights, senses, memories, feelings, actions, behaviours and interests. Experience is full of these events and they will continue. Constant throughout them all, whatever they are, is the state of being, the presence, by which all these experiences are seen and felt and in which they take place. In the same way that this presence is always there, it is there now, in this second, as without it you would not exist. We may call it the state of existence, the presence of being awake, the knowing power, the feeling I, the radiance of the Self, the immediate and direct subject, life. It is this that you are, and not the sense of separate person to which you temporarily identify. In fact that sense of person is a shadow and is not real.

This presence is familiar to you, it is welcome, it is secure, direct and intimate. You do not see it and cannot find it because it is not an object to find, see or feel, it is the presence of the subject. It is the stillness when the mind stops, it is acceptance, it is being who you are and seeing what you are not. It is that which gives you the feeling and conviction I exist.

Becoming increasingly able to recognise this state, to be as it is, is the practice of Atma Vichara. It takes some patience, some persistence, some faith, some guidance and some encouragement. Through the methods of *satyam-yogam-guram-sangham* increasingly the acceptance and recognition of the presence of the radiance I, becomes more tangible and is present as a current of self-awareness, as *Sphurana*. It is then a conviction and no longer assailable by doubt.

So in this moment turn your attention to the presence I, the state of being which you already are. Do not seek for something else; do not probe for some other event. Apply the 3 keys: Who am I? Who knows these thoughts? From where has this I arisen? In this way surrender the mind, rest the mind, into the beauty and presence of that which you already are, the radiance of I and the source from which it has come – heart.

All around and within you, life in all its wonder and creativity will display and move as nature stretches her beauty and potential. It will continue like this with you playing out the destiny of your human part until this body ends. You are not the doer of these actions, nature (shakti) is, you do not die when the body dies. You witness the beautiful rise and the beautiful fall, you are the beautiful, shining intimacy of I and not what you think you have become. In increasingly knowing this, your life, your actions, your speech, your touch and your death will add to this sweetness.

All is well.

The foundations of sadhana

When the student is ready teachings arrive

The foundation of sadhana within which you can now proceed can be stated as six fold:

- **Study** the guidance within this book and the teachings referred to, investigate them earnestly. If they appeal to you, if they awaken your interest, then deepen your understanding and adopt them as your chosen sadhana

- **Have** a relationship with a teacher in one of the ways described

- **Practice** with patience, persistence and gladness as your skill and current develops

- **Belong** and participate in sangha

- **Take** satsang with your teacher when you can

- **Live** ordinarily in the world. Make no special changes – act and work as things come

Om Arunachala Shivaya Namaha
Om Namo Bhagavate Sri Ramanayam

As per the timeless yoga tradition of guram, sangham and satsang, where individuals have a keen need for guidance, and put earnest effort into acquiring this it will be freely and gladly provided. There are numerous sources; where relevant the described arrangements of Yogaliving are accessible to those who choose to seek them out.

A poem's voice

Seeker's Mercy

Shakti moves in earth and sky
Bringing light and beauty to these eyes
Through senses keen and mind alive
Rising up as me and mine

For a million years this common state
Has caused this me to direct its fate
Not knowing directing has always been done
By shakti's power in the fuel of the sun

Whilst thinking and doing, play with flair
Giving fragrance and beauty to this air we share
Thinker and doer, such an elegant potion
Is now revealed as no more than notion

Through it all, through this and that
The light of I shines whole, intact
In love and radiance without need to try
I am that, I do not die

Come to me those who seek
And lay your seeking at these feet
Truth in you will be revealed
With nothing, nothing left concealed

I am sadhana, guru's grace
Who put the Vedas into place
Always existing in time and space
To shine upon the seeker's face

Together taking tentative steps
That weave the maze of karma's debts
Growing in stature through the years
To giant leaps that stride and steer

When student is ripe, teacher arrives
Perhaps appearing unrecognised
With treasured guidance, never random
Satyam, yogam, guram, sangham

Embrace it well as those before
Let practice and teacher frame the door
And courage tread the uneven floor
'Til heart reveals the smooth bright shore

All's well and right just as it is
God's own time will build the bridge
Whilst ego's plans and dreams and hopes
Are little more than clouds and smoke

Be here now, as I in me
Enjoy this life effortlessly
See beauty in you and all other things
As abidance of I where this heart sings

Derek Thorne
Stoer Lodge
Scotland
Autumn 2004

Annexes

Annex 1

The meaning of *Sphurana*

The term *Sphurana* is an obscure Sanskrit word. It was used occasionally by Sri Ramana Maharshi to be descriptive of the current of the heart. It is chosen for the title of this book as it encapsulates profoundly the essence, fabric, direction and outcome of practice.

Sphurana can be formally translated as:

Vibration

Shining

Flashing

Glittering

Emanating

It is also sometimes defined as penetration. When these translations are combined we come closer to the real insight of the word:

The penetration, or the coming in, of vibration.

In yoga texts *Sphurana* is sometimes combined with the term *aham* (which means I am) as in aham sphurana. Its meaning is then lifted into the context that gives the profound communication that is intended here. Shining or flashing can then be applied specifically to the direct personal experience. Now *Sphurana* means something very special indeed, something very revealing for the seeker.

It can now be translated as:

Flashing on the mind, arising or coming into view.

As explained throughout this book, that which is flashing or shining, is the heart. In this way *Sphurana* is the shining of the heart, revealing in the perception of the mind. It is the felt radiance of the Self, appearing and coming into view; in just the same way as the dawn rises and brings the day.

Interestingly, the non-sanskrit word spurana was also in use in Etruscan society in the first millennium BCE. To them it was a municipal word meaning "of the city" or "at the centre".

All the teaching of Atma Vichara, as you will discover through study and practice, relates to hridayam, the heart or source of I, the centre of being. Truly the city or centre that radiates, flashes and shines on the perceiving screen of the personal mind, lighting it to the realisation of the non-personal Self as I.

Annex 2

The historical origins of Atma Vichara

Yoga is very old indeed; it has fuelled peoples' interest for millennia. *Jnana* represents its earliest origins. To find out who we are as our eternal being, and to break free from the confining identity of the ego is jnana. Seeing this and describing this clearly, is the essence of *vedanta* routed in the written form of the *Vedas*, followed by the Upanishads, the Bhagavad Gita and a range of other texts. We do not know for sure how old the Vedas are but it seems they were probably constructed around 3000 BCE. The Upanishads that followed them were created at various times from 1500 BCE onwards. There is little doubt that the oral traditions from which these documents emerged, track back into our ancient and primeval history. It is a marvellous contribution of these enduring teachings that they explain the union of *Atman* and *Brahman* to be the union between the felt individual spirit and the universal spirit or God. This union we can understand as merging as being one, taking place within the immediacy and directness of our own consciousness and not in any external realm.

Jnana yoga as a term is mentioned in the Bhagavad Gita written around 300 BCE. It is the way previously referred to and outlined in the Upanishads. Atma Vichara, enquiring into the Self is the most important meditation practice of jnana yoga. It seems that its application may have varied over time, and in the upanishadic past it was based on pursuing the meditation I am Brahman or I am that or I am not this.

In modern times the immense force of Sri Ramana Maharshi refreshed this ancient current of practice, and made a unique contribution in re-emphasising the sadhana of Atma Vichara as "Who am I?" and promoting it as accessible for the householder as well as the renunciate or the ascetic.

Sri Ramana Maharshi can be seen as part of a long lineage of jnana yoga teaching. Each teacher develops different specific ways, but the essential teachings are those of ancient vedantic philosophy, interpreted amid a re-stating of earlier traditions that have roots stretching back to the early vedic writings and the prehistory of *shiva*.

As we sit and practice today, there is no doubt that we are replicating an authentic jnana yoga sadhana supported by an unbroken current that is as fresh in this modern society and life style as it was in the forest ashrams of the upanishadic era. This long lineage can be both respected and embraced by you, as it is and has been by numerous others who have similarly felt like you. The coming together now of teacher and student in satsang, has we know, been taking place for at least five thousand years and will continue on and on like this.

Annex 3

Sri Ramana Maharshi

A short history

Sri Ramana Maharshi was born in 1879 in the South Indian state of Tamil Nadu with the ordinary Indian name Venkataraman. Following an apparently ordinary childhood, he spontaneously experienced a striking and dramatic awakening at aged sixteen years resulting in direct and permanent realisation of the Self. After a few weeks he walked out of his family home and schoolboy life, under a compulsion to go to the ancient holy temple town of Tiruvannamalai, built around the sacred mountain of Arunachala.

On arrival he renounced everything, became mute, retreated into the temple and withdrew entirely in the immersion of the Self. In recognition of his unique and obvious status, one or two people started to care for him and eventually he became resident in a simple cave ashram on the mountain side, along with a very small group of followers.

As these early years passed, from a position of being almost entirely silent, he began to respond to questions put to him by followers and visitors. The purity and brilliance of his state and of his direct teaching was quickly recognised, and in 1907 Ganapati Muni, a prominent religious scholar and respected local figure, gave him the name Bhagavan Sri Ramana Maharshi.

Those early responses to questions were captured by his key followers and became the written texts of his teachings. These are actually very sparse and few in number but truly brilliant in their clarity and authentic power.

Sri Ramana led a very simple and humble life whilst around

him his fame and popularity grew, leading to a move to a larger yet still discreet mountainside ashram, where he lived for several years with his core band of followers and supporters. In 1922 they all moved to a site at the base of the mountain which became the much larger Sri Ramanasramam, still existing and thriving today.

For fifty years Sri Ramana sat daily in the simple sadhana hall where the Vedas were chanted and where an endless stream of visitors came and sat in his presence. He was often silent but also spoke in answer to questions. Either through silence or through his verbalised responses, peoples' doubts were cleared and many stories exist of the power, purity and grace of his influence.

When he was dying Sri Ramana said:

"They say I am dying but I am not going away, where could I go? I am here."
                                        Sri Ramana Maharshi

Without doubt Sri Ramana represented the manifestation of a guru lineage. Many consider that whilst alive, he was the true embodiment of Dakshinamurti (a form of Shiva) which the mountain Arunachala is itself considered to contain. Since his death in 1950 his potent transference of influence of the timeless current of jnana yoga remains both active, accessible and compelling for those whose heart draws them to it. As the Katha Upanishad says:

"The Self can be attained only by those whom the Self chooses, verily unto them does the Self reveal himself."
                                        Katha Upanishad Part 2 v.23
                                        (Easwaran page 87)

Or as Sri Ramana says:

"Sadhana is like being in the jaws of the tiger's mouth."
                                        Sri Ramana Maharshi

He meant by this that once the attraction is established and the interest and motivation fixed, then the outcome is definite, undeniable and cannot fail.

Anyone with an interest can easily discover more about Sri Ramana's teaching through his works referenced in Annex 9 or by accessing the Ashram's official website at: www.ramana-maharshi.org

Annex 4

The warrior yogi

A message from a warrior to a warrior

Practical life is most problematic when demands, encounters, responsibilities and the need for actions extend beyond our zone of comfort, when we are put in situations that are not easy to solve, or where the prompting of events causes the rising of awkward feelings and unwelcome reactions.

These are all traps of psychology, characteristics of conditioning, but that's what the ego is; memory, desire and conditioned responses. These characteristics race and rush through the emotional plane and the commentating mind, creating a full experience of attraction and aversion, moulding our behaviour accordingly.

The ordinary path is to attempt to effect and shape experience, so that comforts are accentuated and discomforts avoided, thereby retaining the perspective and conditioning by which capabilities are shaped. This trend to stay within the limit of attraction and to resist aversion is confining, limiting us to repeat old habits again and again.

In contrast, the path of the warrior yogi is to persist and endure through what comes, through chaos and through pleasure, through exposure to the difficult as well as the easy, through the arising of limitations and barriers, and getting beyond their influence by allowing their discomfort and seeing through it.

This refusal to be confined by comforts disguised in the ego's play, and to place all effort in the breaking free of its limits and traps, defines the warrior yogi. You need to be a warrior to transcend the influence of the superficial; you need effort to start but not to finish.

Nonetheless, there is a nervous system, there is a physiology, and there is a biological sensing instrument which absolutely deserves care. The path of punishing austerity is a proven barren road. The path of indulgent self-interest, a soft and sad imprisonment. The middle way is the way where sleep, rest, diet, exercise and not consistently overworking, is applied. The path of Atma Vichara can be adopted alongside any approach to sensible health and fitness to achieve that positive, middle way of compassionate, lively and cheerful practical living.

If this teaching of Atma Vichara remains as concept however, then all that happens is that the person walks around with a different concept but nothing really changes. Moving from that position to a practice that is tangible, direct and embedded in felt experience may involve numerous frustrations, and satisfaction may appear elusive. This process however will have to be lived through, and this living through is the province of warriors.

The pace and degree of realisation is not a matter of choice, effort or prediction. It is a matter for destiny. All we can do is surrender to the current and live from the joy of that. Living a life courageously and enthusiastically, where the personality continues to act and play, but identification is no longer there, in the presence of tremendous energy, happiness and spacious vision is achievable for those who try.

Annex 5

Who am I?

It appears that:

There is an actor/doer
There is a thinker   Personalised as me
There is a knower

The truth is:

There is acting
There is thinking   Happening by itself
There is knowing

You are:

Before all experienced objects

Not the body

Not the senses

Not the thoughts

Not the agent of thoughts

Not the thinker

You are the subject, awareness, formless consciousness, in which the agent of thinking, all manifestation and all other experience spontaneously ocurs.

Annex 6

The spheres of recognition

- Only this moment exists

- The display of this moment is perpetual and spontaneous

- I exist and know this moment

- The content of the moment changes, I does not

- I is the spaciousness of being, within which all moves

- This spaciousness is love and freedom

- You are that spaciousness

- You are that love and freedom

- Be that

Annex 7

Yogaliving sutra

- You already exist now as your true nature but you do not see or know it

- This fact is the cause of desire, loneliness and fear

- Your true nature is love, freedom and peace, knowing it, is what you want

- Knowing it, is not found through the actions of doing or thinking

- Knowing it, is being as it

- Learning what this means and relaxing into that learning is sadhana

- Through application, patience and grace, realisation emerges as the dawn rising

- That which obscures the dawn is the identification "I am this person" who thinks and does

- That which reveals the dawn is the radiance of the heart when this identification is dropped

- There is a clear route to bringing this about, it is called Atma Vichara

- It can be taught, learned and applied

- It can be adopted and pursued by anyone who sincerely chooses

- It is the end of seeking and guru's grace

Annex 8

What does it all mean?

So what does it all mean?

It means this:

The world, the universe and life is all one. It has arisen spontaneously, is taking care of itself and is beautiful. Your own life is being lived automatically through this power. It must be as it is now, and must become, as it is destined to change. Accept it and enjoy it as it is.

Despite how it has appeared, you are not the personalised doer or thinker. That assumed identity does not exist. The intimacy of thinking and doing in you, along with everything else, is happening all by itself.

You are the love, the peace and the awareness that shines now and always as I, in which thinking, doing and everything else arises and automatically moves. The coming clear of that fact (the *Spurhana*) is realisation.

Let good action flows through you as work and productivity in the world, relax and allow emerging realisation to shine ever brightly. Do this through patient, ongoing and long term sadhana, through relationship with your teacher and glad fellowship in the community of practitioners. Expect this to continue throughout your whole life.

You are the Self, now and always; be that, live as that.

Be happy as you are and leave behind what you have become.

Annex 9

Recommended texts

The world is full of an endless variety of books containing diverse opinions, perspectives and advice. In the study of yoga there is a risk of dilution and confusion. To support the practical teaching of Atma Vichara given here, only a limited core reference library is necessary. In my opinion the works outlined below constitute such a library. There are many versions and commentaries particularly of the original texts, and of course different interpretations will appeal to different people. Nonetheless in the adjoining bibliography, I have offered my own recommendations and given the publishing information of all the works where that is not detailed here. You can trust these works which will reveal increasing levels of meaning in repeated readings throughout your life.

Original texts

The Upanishads

The Bhagavad Gita

Self-Knowledge (Atma Bodha) of Sri Sankaracarya

Vivekachudamuni of Sri Sankaracarya

The key texts of Sri Ramana Maharshi

Sri Ramana is the source reference for the practice of Atma Vichara. His original texts are direct and essential for mature sadhana but they were compiled in turn of the century rural India and can be a little difficult to assimilate. That is where commentaries are useful for accessibility and understanding. Eventually the original texts become transparent and complete in themselves and ironically commentaries fade away but this probably requires some acclimatisation. Don't be put off, and consider the notes under the "Be as you are" reference given below.

The Collected Works

This small volume contains all the text Sri Ramana ever gave or wrote, which in themselves are slight. It also contains edited versions of Vivekachudamuni and Atma Bodha so is a very useful compilation. However the translations will not appeal to all and may need to be supplemented. In particular I would recommend owning the additional version of Sri Ramanas work Satdarshanam with the brilliant commentary by Natarajan as in the detail listed below.

Satdarshanam

Ramana Maharshi, commentary by A.R. Natarajan, Ramana Maharshi Centre for Learning, Bangalore, India.
ISBN 8185378-15-0

Ramana Gita – Dialogues with Sri Ramana Maharshi

This is not contained within the collected works as it was not directly written by Ramana but approved by him and compiled by his devotee, senior associate and scholar Ganapati Muni. It contains beautiful material as the original was compiled in precise Sanskrit. It is also the source in chapter 2 verse 2 of the immensely profound heart sloka quoted above on page 26.

Written records of satsang given by Sri Ramana Maharshi

Talks with Sri Ramana Maharshi

This is an extensive record of question and answer originally given by Sri Ramana in satsang within the visitors' hall at Sri Ramanasramam. It has got everything recorded in it with little attempt to edit; therefore it contains excellent gems amid less useful inclusions. However, satsang can in reality often be like this and the book gives the reader a good cultural flavour of the experience of the time.

Be As You Are – The Teachings of Sri Ramana Maharshi

This is an excellent compilation and regrouping of the original talks, it is very accessible and the best introduction. This is the easy reading book I would advise beginners or simply the curious to use.

The key satsang text of Sri Nisargadatta Maharaj

I Am That

A unique and classic work by this outstanding and original teacher, who was a contemporary of Sri Ramana Maharshi but who had a radically different and often challenging style of delivering satsang. The power and confrontation of his incisive style is remarkable, and this volume retains a very real energy to provoke insight, in much the same way as the experiences reported in his small Bombay satsang room. There is little consideration for sensibilities, just direct communication of truth. This provides a raw but startling beauty.

Glossary

Aham – I am

Ahimsa – Non-harming

Arjuna – The prince in the story of the Bhagavad Gita whom Krishna instructs in spiritual knowledge

Asana – "Seat" most commonly used to mean posture in hatha yoga

Ashram – "Hermitage" an environment for spiritual study and practice

Atma Vichara – Self-enquiry

Atman – The spiritual Self

Brahman – The absolute, the totality of all

Dharma – The natural order of things

Dhyana – Meditation

Guru/Guram – That which dispels darkness – spiritual teacher

Hatha – Forceful, physical yoga

Hridayam – Spiritual heart, the centre, the source

Jnana – Knowledge, wisdom or insight

Jnani – One established in jnana

Karma – Conditioning

Karma Yoga – Selfless service

Kundalini – The shakti of transformation

Nadi Shodhana – A pranayama practice

Neti – Not this

Niyama – Moral conduct through restraint as defined in Patanjali's Yoga Sutras

Sadhak – Spiritual practitioner, aspirant

Sadhana – Spiritual practice

Sangha/Sangham – Community of spiritual practitioners

Sanskrit – The original language of the Vedas and the common language of yoga

Satchitananda – Being – consciousness – joyful peace

Satsang – The company of the wise – spiritual discourse with your teacher

Satyam – Truth

Seva – Service

Shakti – Power, energy

Shiva – God

Sloka – Verse

Sutra – "Thread" – the precise essence of teaching

Sphurana – See Annex 1

Tapas – "Heat" most often used as an alternative term for sadhana.

Upanishad – "Sitting down near" – with the teacher, a set of vedantic teachings

Vasanas – Desires

Vedanta – "Vedas end" – the philosophical teachings expressed in the Upanishads, Bhagavad Gita etc

Veda – "Knowledge" – the original and ancient Hindu texts

Yama – Moral conduct through observance as defined in Patanjali's Yoga Sutras

Yogam – Yoga

Yoga Nidra – "Yogic sleep" a particular yoga practice of deep relaxation

Yogi – A practitioner of Yoga

Bibliography

Easwaran Eknath. *The Bhagavad Gita.* Arkana Publication, 1986.

Easwaran Eknath. *The Upanishads.* Arkana Publications, 1988.

Ed. Fleming Ursula. *Meister Eckhart.* Fount Publications, 1988.

Ed. Godman David. *Be As You Are – The Teachings of Sri Ramana Maharshi.* Penguin, 1992.

Prabhavananda Swami. *Shankara's Crest – Jewel of Discrimination (Viveka – Chudamani).* Vedanta Press, 1947.

Natarajan A.R. *Ramana Gita – Dialogues with Sri Ramana Maharshi.* Bangalore, India. Ramana Maharshi Centre for Learning, 1996.

Nikhilananda Swami. *Self-Knowledge (Atma Bodha) of Sri Sankaracarya.* Mylapore, Chennai, India. Sri Ramakrishna Math, 1947.

Nisargadatta Maharaj. *I Am That.* Translated by Frydman Maurice. Bombay, India. Chetana Press, 1973.

Ramana Maharshi. *The Collected Works.* Tiruvannamalai. Sri Ramanasramam, 1996.

The Yoga Sutras of Patanjali. Numerous versions available.

Venkataramiah Munagala. *Talks with Sri Ramana Maharshi.* Tiruvannamalai. Sri Ramanasramam, 1955.

The Teacher's Farewell

Where shall I go now my teacher?

Go wherever you like

You mean I can do anything?

Yes, except for one thing

What is that?

Don't resist

What must I do to not resist?

Do sadhana, live gladly in love,
acceptance and trust and see
one thing clearly

What must I see?

That there is no-one who resists

I love you my teacher

I love you too